Flying Solo

JULIA WISE

BAAF
ADOPTION
& FOSTERING

Published by
British Association for Adoption & Fostering
(BAAF)
Saffron House
6–10 Kirby Street
London EC1N 8TS
www.baaf.org.uk

Charity registration 275689

British Library Cataloguing in Publication Data
A catalogue record for this book is available from the British
Library

ISBN 978 1 905664 00 9

Photograph on cover posed by models by istockphoto.com,
Helen Joubert and APM Studios
Designed by Andrew Haig & Associates
Typeset by Fravashi Aga, London
Printed in Great Britain by T J International Ltd
Trade distribution by Turnaround Publisher Services, Unit 3,
Olympia Trading Estate, Coburg Road, London N22 6TZ

BAAF is the leading UK-wide membership organisation for all
those concerned with adoption, fostering and child care issues.

Acknowledgements

I am more grateful than I can say for the unfailing love and support of my parents, without which life would be simply impossible. A great thank you also to my friend Annie, who is the best friend anyone could hope for, and her husband Matt, for their endless support, advice and ability to listen. Thanks also to Hedi Argent, without whose sensible advice and patience this book may never have seen the light of day.

All names have been changed for the purpose of publication in order to protect identities – particularly that of my son.

About the author

Julia Wise has been a journalist and TV producer and is now living in East Anglia with her son Alan and Millie the cat and makes a living – well almost – teaching French and doing general supply in local secondary schools.

The Our Story series
This book is one in a new series published by BAAF which explores adoption experiences as told by adoptive parents.

Also available in this series: *An Adoption Diary* by Maria James and *In Black and White* by Nathalie Seymour.

The series editor
Hedi Argent is the editor of this series. She is an independent adoption consultant, trainer and freelance writer. She is the author of *Find me a Family* (Souvenir Press, 1984), *Whatever Happened to Adam?* (BAAF, 1998), *Related by Adoption* (BAAF, 2004), *One of the Family* (BAAF, 2005), *Ten Top Tips for Placing Children in Permanent Families* (BAAF, 2006), the co-author of *Taking Extra Care* (BAAF, 1997), and *Dealing with Disruption* (BAAF, 2006), and the editor of *See you Soon* (BAAF, 1995), *Staying Connected* (BAAF, 2002) and *Models of Adoption Support* (BAAF, 2003). She has also contributed four illustrated booklets to the children's series published by BAAF: *What Happens in Court?* (2003), *What is Contact?* (2004), *What is a Disability?* (2004) and *Life Story Work* (2005) with Shaila Shah.

For Alan

Contents

1

Where's the Daddy?

Sometimes when my seven-year-old son climbs into bed with me in the mornings, and especially if it's after 5.30am and I'm able to speak coherently, we chat. Occasionally we have this conversation:

> *Alan:*   *I wish I had a Daddy.*
>
> *Me:*   *Do you, sweetheart?*
>
> *Alan:*   *Yes, because then I could ride on his shoulders and he could play football with me. Mums are useless at football.*
>
> *Me:*   *That would be nice, wouldn't it? Well perhaps we might find one some day. Would you like that?*
>
> *Alan:*   *Yes, I think so...*
>
> *PAUSE*
>
> *Me:*   *Of course, if we had a Daddy, he would have to sleep in Mummy's bed...*
>
> *PAUSE*
>
> *Alan:*   *Oh! Well, that's okay. You could sleep here and he could sleep there, and I could sleep in the middle!*
>
> *Me:*   *And I'd have to hug him, too, sometimes...*

> *Alan:*   *Hmmm. Why?*
> *Me:*   *Because that's what Mummies and Daddies do. You could hug him too.*
> *PAUSE*
> *Alan:*   *I don't think we really need a Daddy.*

End of conversation.

*   *   *

Before Alan, I was completely used to being on my own. I lived alone, I'd travelled alone, I made virtually all my decisions alone. So making the decision on my own to be a parent didn't strike me as at all weird. In any case, when I first made the decision to adopt, I was concentrating solely on "adopting". Somehow I failed to think far enough ahead to realise truly that I would be a parent on my own, or what that would mean in real terms. Even when I started to attend pre-adoption classes, where everyone else was in couples and I was the only single one, I still didn't really twig. How could I be so dense? Well, like every new parent-to-be, I had no idea what I was doing! When the penny finally dropped, it happened in a single moment. A woman came to talk to our group. We'd all been looking forward to meeting her, because she was "the real thing". She and her husband had adopted a small boy and he'd been living with them for about six months. She showed us pictures, told a few anecdotes. One story in particular (I can't remember the details) was rather sweet and as we reached the "ahhh" moment, I looked up for someone to "ahhh" with and I suddenly realised that, of course, all the couples were "ahhh"-ing together and I had no one to "ahhh" with. It was an important moment of self-realisation in my journey towards single parent adoption (ahhh!).

The adoption agency apologised to me for not being able to provide other potential single adopters to join my group. Perhaps it would have been nice. We, the single parents, could have exchanged glances of horror or sympathy during those moments of truth, perhaps we could have kept in touch afterwards and swapped anecdotes of our own. But actually, being a single person amongst those couples was good training for the future, for nowadays, when we go to school meetings, trips, or on holidays, Alan and I are frequently the only single parent family in an ocean of dual parent families. Don't say "ahhh" this time – I'm mostly comfortable being on my own and that's because now I have friends who are mothers in couples and now, apparently, I know the "truth"...well, several apparent "truths" really, as expressed by married women in my social midst.

The first "truth" is that fathers quite often go out to work at 8am in the morning and don't come home until 7pm, the upshot being that they miss most of the parenting. Furthermore, it appears that when fathers are at home (weekends mostly), 8 times out of 10 they're a) nothing but trouble; b) never do anything useful and if they try to, they do it badly; and c) undermine all the rest of the parenting that's gone on in the week while they've been at work. I would like to add that the above comments in no way reflect my personal views of marriage, fathers or men in general! Indeed, the men I know who stay at home while their partners go out to work full time say similar stuff, it's just that there aren't many of them and they don't tend to hang out with the women. I'm telling you, it's amazing what you can pick up by way of a social education from the odd hour spent at a coffee morning! I certainly had no idea.

Clearly, all this probably owes more to my female friends' chronic lack of sleep (something I know a lot about) than to the TRUTH as such, though in short, and all things considered, I have now concluded that two parents are not always better than one!

Still, you don't have to be the brain of Britain to

understand that there are definite advantages in having two adults around the place and I would be lying if I didn't confess that I, too, sometimes wished we had a Daddy. Would I like some handsome, intelligent, strong knight in shining armour to come galloping up, scoop me up in his arms and take the weight of the world off my shoulders? You bet I would! Someone to share the highs and lows, to share the chores, to share child-time, to share adult-time, to share discipline, to take over when the ends of tethers are reached, to be in when the other is out and so on and so on. When you're outside family life and looking in, you can see and know intellectually that this is important, but you don't really SEE and KNOW anything until you're on the inside.

So why did I decide to adopt a child on my own? The obvious question, you might think, but not one that I'm generally asked, though I'm constantly amazed at how intrusive people feel they can be about Alan and his life story. When they discover I adopted Alan on my own they often ask how it was possible, since they've usually heard how hard it is to adopt. But I can't remember anybody ever asking me what made me do it. My theory is that they feel the territory might be just slightly too dodgy, perhaps they fear the possible can of emotional worms it might open up. After all, I'm a single woman, headed for middle age; my life revolved around my work and I was living alone in a one-bedroom flat before the adoption ... do you recognise me? I'm that rather sad and needy figure of fun that's appeared in many sitcoms and soaps over the years! I've seen the look on people's faces that says 'I don't want to go there!' whenever I may have seemed about to explain myself. Women – some women – can't really understand why I would want to live without a man. Some men, I think, assume I must be a kind of man-hating lesbian. As for me, I don't particularly care what anyone thinks, which is one reason, I suppose, why I went through with it.

I worked very hard in my career and didn't meet anybody I wanted to spend the rest of my life with – it was just one of those things. And then one morning, just before Christmas, about 12 years ago, I woke up ill. We had had a works do at a posh restaurant in West London. There had been dancing and a conga line, I recall, although like nearly everyone else, I was fairly full of Christmas cheer and the details are somewhat fuzzy. The next morning I awoke feeling slightly hung-over, but perfectly fit for work. During that morning, in fact in the middle of a meeting, I began to feel very unwell. Somehow I could tell that this "unwell" was something serious. I had stomach pains, I started to vomit – I got sent home in a car. I didn't go back to work for another three months. It transpired, after a couple of weeks of being literally at death's door and not being able to get a satisfactory diagnosis, that my bowel had become obstructed and I was admitted to hospital for emergency surgery. I was in a terrible state by the time I reached Accident and Emergency and hardly fit for an operation. The surgeons were not sure what they would find when they opened me up. They sent the cancer nurse to tell me that cancer was the most common reason for a bowel obstruction and that when I came round from the operation I would probably find myself with a colostomy. They sent the anaesthetist to tell me that there was a chance I might not survive the anaesthetic but that the surgeon had insisted the operation should go ahead immediately. They made me sign a piece of paper to say that I understood the risks.

My parents and some of my friends came rushing to my side, but I was very much concerned that they should not be made to worry any more than necessary, so I kept the details to myself. I remember feeling tremendously unwell, with a tube down my throat into my stomach, and cramping pains in my abdomen. I also remember saying to myself I WILL NOT die! Whether this helped or not, I don't know, but in any case, I didn't die and there was no need for a colostomy.

Fortunately, the surgeon was right to operate. He saved my life. When they opened me up they found that scar tissue had grown inside me and it had somehow twisted my bowel, presumably during the rather energetic Conga dance at the office party – who says exercise is good for you!

It was following this trauma and with a new sense of my own strength of character that I started to look at my life and see the holes. After the operation I had three months to convalesce, during which time I watched a lot of TV. Hours and hours of watching fairly pointless and completely forgettable television was enough to make me wonder at the futility of the hours and hours of my life I spent making fairly pointless and completely forgettable television programmes, often with some rather unpleasant people. When I was well, I went back to work reluctantly and started to look for ways to improve my life. I looked ahead and realised that if I didn't do something I would end up miserable and alone. I began to realise that what was missing in my life was a family – children. Then I discovered, quite by chance, that I might be able to adopt a child on my own. I knew that I was in a position financially to set myself up so that I would at least be able to make ends meet for a few years. I thought it through. I made a choice and happily my joyful child reminds me daily that it was the right choice, not only for me, but also for him.

I know now that when I made this momentous decision, thinking in my self-centred way that it would only affect me and a child, I had in fact made a decision that would change the lives of everyone close to me, my parents in particular. As it was, I fairly tactlessly made the announcement in this conversation with my mother:

    Me: *Listen, I've rung to tell you about something*

I've decided.

Mum: *Oh yes, what's that? (thinking, I guess, that I was going to tell them where I was going on holiday)*

Me: *I've decided that I'm going to adopt a child.*

Mum: *(Silence)*

Me: *I've thought it through and it's possible.*

Mum: *I see. (more silence)*

Me: *Well, what do you think?*

Mum: *I don't know.*

Me: *(getting impatient) It's not that outrageous. Lots of people do it. (Oh yeah?)*

Mum: *Well, I don't really know what to say, dear.*

Me: *OK, well look, I just wanted to tell you. I'll talk to you soon.*

* * *

Not exactly the reaction I was hoping for! In fact, about 10 minutes later my Mum called me back and apologised for not being more receptive – although there was no need to apologise. After all, I had just dropped the most enormous bombshell. She said, in true "my Mum" style, that of course they would support me, as they had always supported me and that they would help me in any way. Looking back, I don't think I deserved such generosity, but I'm grateful for it all the same.

Of course, decision or no decision, it didn't just depend on me. Like all potential adopters, except perhaps Madonna, I had a lengthy process of training and approval to go through. I recently asked my social worker what it was about me that made him think I could make this work:

Me: *What made you think I would be able to cope with being a single adopter?*

Sam: *It's hard to explain. There is a sort of commonality amongst people that you feel are suitable to adopt. It's an ability to be able to*

> *grasp the reality of the situation, I think. The way that they're able to unpick their own lives and experiences during the approval process, for example, is a good indication that they will be able to build something new and positive when they become adopters. We're never looking for perfect parents as such. But I very much felt that you seemed able to project into the future what you were going to need to do. And you showed commitment – quite early on you sold your flat and bought the house near your parents, because you had obviously taken on board what you were learning and understood what you needed to do.*

Me: *What about during the group sessions?*

Sam: *It was important to see how you interacted with others and how you were able to get on with them. Basically, I was looking for someone who was quite together and stable and you were definitely that.*

*   *   *

Well, it's nice to know someone thinks so! But I have to admit, there are times when I have been close to the edge – like most parents – because children, I've discovered, know how to find all the right buttons to push. It's at times like those that I appreciate having my feet on the ground and having my support team just round the corner.

So what's it like being a single adopter in everyday life? Most of the time, we're just an ordinary family. Alan has been in preschool and now school with the same group of children since he was three. They take us for granted. Some of the mothers have become good friends. Ultimately, though, when we get home at the end of the day and the doors are shut, it's just me and Alan.

We have routines – when Alan came to me he was

desperate for routine – and I try to keep these going. In fact, I rather overcompensate. We always eat together – I try to lay the table properly for every meal, so that we have a reason to sit down together like a family, small though we are, and I try to organise time for us to do things together. I clean his shoes every day. We're never late for school. I make the beds every morning, even if the rest of the house is a tip. Oh dear! This is starting to sound rather obsessive, but these are the things that help me feel that we're still OK, whilst acknowledging that the world doesn't grind to a halt if I don't get them done.

Alan would like me to play with him more, and I do try every day, but there is stuff I have to do – cooking, washing up, cleaning, tidying, gardening ... there's no division of labour here. I cop the lot. When Alan's in bed, I'm often too whacked to catch up on chores that I've missed. It can pile up. I watch too much TV. I worry about money. I worry about Alan's behaviour. I comfort eat. There's no one to take my side, like in 'Don't talk to your mother like that!' or 'Didn't your mother tell you to get into bed?' Does all this sound dreadful? If so, then it sounds worse than it feels. It's just life going on. Perhaps if I'd KNOWN about it before I had Alan, I might have balked at it, although now I'm here, oddly I seem to be happy. I have wondered, though, why my married friends with children didn't warn me off. I asked my friend Sarah, one of my referees:

> Me: *Why didn't you tell me what being a parent was really like?*
>
> Sarah: *There's no point. You wouldn't have believed me.*
>
> Me: *Possibly, but you still felt you could recommend me?*
>
> Sarah: *I was sure you didn't know what you were letting yourself in for, but then neither did we when we first had children. The thing is, until you have children of your own you can't really*

understand the emotional pressures of it. I was
confident you'd be fine, because I know you well
and I know you have plenty of inner stamina!

Inner stamina? Sounds more like a breakfast cereal than a state of mind (I'll take a bowl of inner stamina, please!), but if she meant "bloody-minded", then I dare say I'd have to agree.

* * *

Which brings me on to the subject of prejudice. I haven't been aware of much prejudice towards me as a single mother. Obviously, most people in my circle know that I have adopted Alan on my own. But not everybody does, and I imagine some people assume I'm either divorced or just not married. Am I more or less acceptable because I made myself a single parent on purpose? I'm not sure. I know that within children's services, where there is now a general acceptance of single adoption as a viable option for some children, there are still mixed attitudes. I nearly lost Alan at one point because of a change in personnel. His first social worker was very happy with me as a potential parent for Alan. When she suddenly left and a young man took her place, he was no longer happy, and started searching for two adoptive parents for Alan all over again. This delayed the whole process by about six months, which was not good for Alan, and was frustrating for me. After a few months, he also left and Alan's original social worker returned and it was back to the beginning with me once more. In the real world, attitudes are also mixed I think, although no one has ever expressed any negative views to my face.

As a singleton I don't get invited to dinner or to parties much (to my intense relief in many cases!). That might just be because I'm boring or otherwise anti-social, but I think it's more likely because I don't have a partner. I'm the spare wheel at family barbecues. I find it hard to go out in the week because I have to find a babysitter, which is difficult and anyway I can't really afford it, so eventually people stop asking. Very few mothers – but these are the ones whose tea I should like to poison – don't feel able to let their children play at our house. I guess we'll always be a little "Not Quite Like Us" to some. Still, nil desperandum. It's not like me to give up the ghost, socially or otherwise. I started a book group, which met monthly at my house (if you can't take Mohammed to the mountain...). I joined the pre-school committee. I became involved in Beavers (baby Cubs) when Alan was old enough to join. I edged my way into village life and I simply decided I would have no truck with any attitudes I felt were unhelpful to Alan, and that was that!

Of course, it's all very well for me to turn my nose up and turn my back on people unwilling to accept my lifestyle, but it's not so easy for Alan. Although he would find it hard to accept a new person coming into our lives and possibly taking some of my attention away from him, I know he does sometimes seriously feel the lack of a Daddy. So much so that occasionally he ventures into the world of fantasy to provide one. For instance, for several weeks he believed, sincerely I think, that Jeff Tracy from the Thunderbirds was his real father and that he, Alan, was in fact Alan Tracy. He would refer to Jeff as 'my dad' and even went so far as to suggest that I had been killed in an avalanche, which is what happened to the absent Mrs Tracy in the story!

Just the other day I had this conversation with a friend whose daughter Helen is in Alan's class at school. We were standing at the gate, waiting for the children to come out:

Christine:	*By the way, Julia, Helen told me something interesting about Alan the other day.*
Me:	*(slightly nervous) Oh really? What was that?*
Christine:	*Well, Helen said Alan told her that his father*

> *was in the army but that he'd been killed fighting. Helen told me because she was confused – she said she thought Alan didn't have a Daddy.*

Me: *(trying not to show my horror) Ah…Oh dear! I wonder what brought that on. Thanks for telling me, Chris.*

Christine: *That's OK. I thought you might be interested. They were probably playing some army game or something.*

Me: *Oh yes, probably.*

*   *   *

I think I was quite cool about it outwardly, although I felt bad, as I always do when I hear that Alan has been telling stories like this. I very gently brought the subject up and Alan quite matter-of-factly explained, 'Well, they asked me about my Dad, and I had to say something!' And I know exactly what he means. The kids are curious. Why not give them something to think about? I'm reminded of an incident when Alan was very small and we had one of his friends round to play. The little friend looked all around the house, ticking off all that was both familiar and unfamiliar in our home. After a while, and looking a little confused, he came up to me and asked, 'Where's the Daddy?' A good question and one that deserves a good and creative answer!

2

Whose idea was it to get a cat?

We got the cat in response to Alan's constant pleas for a dog, on the basis that cats are more independent and can look after themselves a lot of the time (who was I kidding?!). We had already had two goldfish – Alan has had a lifelong (so far) interest in things fishy – whom we named Spot (it had a large, black spot on its side which contrived to disappear a few weeks after we'd named him, making the name seem somewhat eccentric) and Mango, which is Maori for shark. Alan loved these goldfish so much, he really wanted to hug them and stroke them, as you would with a cat or dog; and in spite of my frequent interventions and attempts to explain about the differences between fish and cats, I would occasionally find Alan, smiling and wet-handed, with a tell-tale puddle around the base of the tank, indicating that he had succeeded in "cuddling" either Mango or Spot before I could stop him. Despite this, the fish survived remarkably well for a couple of years, when they finally, and rather suddenly, succumbed to some invisible infection and were discovered one morning fins up and motionless at the top of the tank. Cowardly in the face of a perplexed and slightly wobbly Alan, I explained that the fish needed to go to the vet, from whence, I have to admit, they never returned. At the time, Alan did not question this explanation but out of the blue, just the other day, and three years on, he suddenly blurted out in the car on the way to school, 'You know the goldfish that went to the vet, Mum? They died, didn't they?' 'Yes, I'm afraid so,' I replied. 'Oh, I thought so,' he shrugged, and no more was said.

Anyway, after the sad and sort of secret demise of Spot and Mango, I made the decision to get the cat. Now, I'd never had a cat before and am not a great lover of cats, but I felt adding one to the household might help swell the ranks of our tiny family, or at least give the illusion of it. We took several trips to the Animal Sanctuary and finally picked Millie, a pretty gingery tabby cat. As far as Alan was concerned, it worked:

> Alan: *We've got a big family, haven't we, Mummy? There's you and me and Grandma and Grandad and Uncle John (my brother) and Spot and Mango ("at the vet's") and Millie. That's lots!*

* * *

But although Millie fulfilled a need, she failed to perform in certain key areas. At the rescue centre they assured us that Millie "liked" children. I now understand this to mean that she wouldn't bite, scratch or otherwise attack Alan, unless provoked, but that under no circumstances would she stay in the same room as him, or allow him to touch or stroke her, unless restrained. Most of the time, Alan was able to be quite philosophical about this situation, though he longed to play with her. But it could be a source of misery. I remember on one occasion meeting a sobbing Alan on the stairs. He was wearing one rubber glove and carrying a pair of tweezers!

> *Me:*   *Alan, what's the matter darling?*
>
> *Alan:*   *Millie (sniff) won't – play – with – me! And she scratched me!*

Now, I had no idea what diabolical game Alan had been attempting to "play", so though I felt badly for my bereft son, and attempted to comfort him, I secretly sympathised with poor Millie, who had no doubt narrowly escaped with her dignity intact.

*   *   *

During weekend training courses arranged by my agency, before I was approved to adopt, there was much talk about support networks. We were advised to take this extremely seriously and I began to think it through well in advance of any final decisions. Experience now tells me that for single adopters, particularly, this is such a vital issue. In fact, recently I was asked to talk to a group of potential adopters, many of whom were single, and I felt I had to say that without a solid support network, forget it! Very early on in the process, the adoption agency (who've only dealt with a dozen or so single adopters in the past 25 years) put me in touch with a woman who'd adopted a boy on her own about a year previously. When I called her, she was just opening a bottle of wine (my kind of person, I thought!) and it was helpful to talk to someone who was dealing with the very same problems I was about to encounter and who told the truth:

> *Carol:* *This is a peaceful time of night – when my son is in bed. I quite often have a glass of wine and just sit and chill out.*
>
> *Me:*   *That sounds like a good idea.*
>
> *Carol:* *Believe me, it's easy to forget that you need to look after yourself as well as your child. It can*

*be very stressful and tiring when you're on your
own. You have to tell yourself that it's OK to
do something just for you.*

Good advice!

*   *   *

My own circumstances were as follows: I was living in
London, working hard and socialising in my free time with
friends, who were also involved in busy careers. I lived in a
one-bedroom flat, which would have been virtually
impossible to extend; in any case, I wouldn't have been able
to afford to extend it or to move to a larger place in
London. My family and my oldest and closest friends lived
miles away in various parts of the country. I realised that if
I was to go through with the adoption, I would have to
move to be nearer to the friends and family I knew I would
be able to depend on. I imagine at this point my London
friends will yell with outrage "Not fair!" But it's not a
criticism. My London friends are lovely, just at different
stages in their lives and busy with it. I think from people, as
from cats, it's unfair to expect more than they can offer.
And so my first move was a physical one – I sold my flat
and bought a house in the country, just a few miles away
from my parents and minutes away from one of my oldest
friends, Annie. It was the best move I ever made!

But what of my potentially long-suffering friend and
family, you may ask. Was this fair to them? That's a good
question, and one I didn't really consider at the time as
much as I should have done, because I didn't really have
any idea of what my needs were going to be or just how
much I would need to depend on them. Recently, I asked
Annie what she felt when she knew I was intending to move
in round the corner with my new family.

> *Me:*   *I never really asked permission or anything
> when I moved into the village and landed*

> *myself and Alan on you. Did you mind?*
>
> *Annie: No – I was looking forward to having you around more often. It was exciting. Obviously we didn't know what to expect with Alan, but I wanted to help you make it work.*
>
> *Me: How do you feel now, in retrospect?*
>
> *Annie: Well, I just think Alan's a very different little boy now from when he first came to live with you. We like having you around, and it's good for Jack and Jamie (Annie's sons) to have a little one around.*
>
> *Me: Do you think I've abused our friendship and imposed too much on you?*
>
> *Annie: Not at all. We've been happy to help out when you've needed us and we've enjoyed having you here to meals and so on. I wish we could have helped more.*

* * *

The implications of moving so far out of London were great. Although I didn't admit it straight away, I knew in my heart of hearts it was the prelude to a major change in lifestyle. It wasn't going to be a case of seamlessly inserting a child into my life and carrying on pretty much as before (how innocent we are when, childless, we contemplate parenthood!). Once I had a child, I knew I would have to give up my job and find an alternative way of making a living. In the run-up to the final adoption, life became very difficult. At first, having sold my flat in town and bought a three-bedroom house with a large garden in the country, I also rented a small flat in London, close to work. It was a nightmare of lost belongings – I could never remember where I'd put anything and what was in which home.

Later on, I gave up the flat in London and commuted every day. It was exhausting! Work became less satisfying as I had less energy to do a good job and weekends were a grind. Work colleagues became less supportive as I appeared to be less productive and more focused on my future. I swear some of them thought I was making the whole adoption thing up! As one project finished, I was moved to a project that I really didn't want to do. So it was a relief almost as much as a surprise when the adoption finally became a reality and I had to drop everything, leave work with hardly any notice and be a Mum.

It's hard to remember, now, the little lad, aged two, I brought home for the first time five years ago. I can't imagine what it must have felt like to that little tot, to be uprooted by a stranger called Mummy and taken to a strange place in the country, when he was used to living in a city with lots of noise and familiar faces around him. His foster home had been pretty chaotic – full of other children with problems. If little Alan had any problems then, they would have been hard to see amongst the hubbub and the to-ings and fro-ings of the household. Unfamiliar though it was, the calm and peace of his new home seemed to be good for Alan. He slept well at night, he ate well, he responded immediately to the introduction of routines and he looked a lot healthier within just a few days. I recall that I felt he really needed a sleep during the day, but he was very resistant, because he wanted to play, so after lunch I would pop him in the car and drive around for an hour or so. He would drop off quickly and sleep for a couple of hours and I would quite enjoy getting to know my way around the area again and visiting old haunts in the car. I remember loving to watch how the countryside changed during that year – something I'd missed when I lived in London. It didn't occur to me that Alan wouldn't also enjoy looking out of the car window during our daily trips, until one day, my little townie son cried rather plaintively as I was putting him in the car, 'Mummy, I HATE fields!'.

The new people in Alan's life, my support group, helped enormously to create a happy and stable life for both of us and in a most unselfish way. Any doubts they may have privately had were set aside. Alan had seen photographs of his new extended family and knew who Grandma and Grandad were and he was very excited about meeting Jack and Jamie, Annie's sons, who he knew had a climbing frame in their garden. He took to Grandma immediately and she to him; but, right from the start, he was hugely impressed by his new Grandad. My father was intially more unsure about the adoption than my mother:

Mum: *Don't mind about your Dad. He worries about you and it's hard for him to envisage what things will be like.*

Me: *Really?*

Mum: *Yes. Men are different to us. They love their own children and would do anything for them, but they can't really understand why you'd want to look after anybody else's!*

* * *

I considered these comments and, while they may not be generally true, or only partly so, they were probably true about my father. I'm sure he was worried, but I was confident he would "come round" and an incident a few days after his first meeting with Alan seemed to do the trick. I took Alan to a local hairdresser's quite near to my parents' home, to get a little trim. My Dad, obviously having heard we would be there, walked past to give us a wave on his way back from shopping. When Alan saw him he was so delighted he shouted, 'That's my Grandad!' at the top of his voice. The whole salon looked and a proud Grandad needed no more convincing. Alan and Grandad are now great friends. My brother, to whom the whole thing must have seemed like a sister's ridiculous whim (OK, I admit to a few whims), just took the whole thing in his stride. He simply accepted Alan as one of the family, accepted that the face of family events would never be the same (perhaps better?), turns up regularly with presents and good humour and puts up with being adored by his new nephew.

So how do these wonderful people figure in our lives and support us every day? Firstly, just knowing they're there and that they care is really helpful. We talk nearly every day (I try not to phone too early!) and I see them several times a week. They drop in. We drop in. They don't care if I haven't tidied up or made the beds (well, my Mum minds, but happily, if she's that bothered she tidies up and makes the beds herself! I can remember when I first left home how territorial I would have been about that sort of "interference". How stupid was I then?!). It has been lovely coming home and being close to my family again. Of course Alan only has one set of grandparents, but I don't have in-laws to contend with, which is perhaps something of an advantage. And then there are the emergencies, although thankfully there haven't been too many of them. For example, the times when Alan has been sick and I've needed some physical as well as emotional support; the time when Alan threw a tantrum of such destructive force that eventually I had to call Annie to come and take him away until we both calmed down enough to be able to clear up the mess; my first day at work, when Alan was ill, and my Mum stepped in at a moment's notice...

There are the everyday routine things, the picking up from school, the odd tenner from my Mum when things get tight, babysitting, sleepovers, listening to me moaning, talking over and over problems with no resolution, putting up with me when I do phone at 8am because I've already been up for hours and have forgotten to check the time... I could go on. I often do! The point is that, as a lone parent, you inevitably need help and sometimes it's hard to ask, even those closest to you, for what you need. Without these people to help us, Alan and I couldn't manage half as well as we do. So does this mean we're not a proper family? No. It means we're a family in the old-fashioned sense – a small unit within an extended family – and we do what we can to give back something in return.

Not only have my parents supported me both practically and morally, but their main support has been the way each has developed a special relationship with my son.

My Dad, now in his 70s, has been able to share one of his lifelong interests with Alan. As a younger man he went fishing a lot. He gave up years ago, but still retained an interest and kept all his fishing tackle, some of which he'd made himself. Alan has always shown an interest in animals and in nature and from somewhere developed this burning desire to go fishing. It became almost obsessive. For a while, we had a conversation something like this practically every night as I tucked him into bed:

> *Alan:*   *Mum, can anyone go fishing?*
>
> *Me:*   *Well, yes. If they know what to do and if they have the right equipment.*
>
> *Alan:*   *Have we got the right equipment, Mummy?*
>
> *Me:*   *We haven't, but I think Grandad has.*
>
> *Alan:*   *Can we go fishing with Grandad?*
>
> *Me:*   *Well, we can ask him if he'd like to.*
>
> *Alan:*   *Can we ask him now?*
>
> *Me:*   *Not right now, darling, it's bedtime.*
>
> *Alan:*   *Can we ask him tomorrow?*
>
> *Me:*   *If you like.*
>
> *Alan:*   *Can we go fishing tomorrow, Mummy?*
>
> *Me:*   *Well...*
>
> *Alan:*   *When can we go fishing, Mummy?*
>
> *Me:*   *W...*
>
> *Alan:*   *I want to go fishing with Grandad tomorrow!*

*   *   *

Eventually, a fishing trip was arranged. It went very smoothly. Alan and his Grandad have now become firm fishing partners and are often to be seen down by the river, where they sit for hours, chatting and watching nature happen and fishing. We marvel, my Mum and I, at how long they manage to stay out, in all weathers. My Dad is amazed at how enthusiastic Alan is and at how skilful he has become. He looks forward to their fishing trips as much, if not more, than Alan.

My Mum and Alan share a birthday. They also, apparently, share a sense of fun. The first time she babysat for me, I arrived home at midnight, Alan was still up and they were still playing. She said, 'He didn't seem to want to go to bed!' She still babysits, but now the novelty's worn off, and routines are more firmly ingrained, she's able to be rather more firm. She also meets Alan from school sometimes when I can't, and when I get home from work or wherever I've been, she's often to be found wielding a sword or pretending to be a horse. She's not averse to the odd bit of football either, despite sore feet and arthritic knees. She's also the secret purveyor of sweets, which she keeps stashed in her handbag! I pretend to disapprove, but actually I'm kind of happy to encourage the sense of conspiracy between them.

Annie and her family too have forged their own relationships with Alan. Her boys are older and he adores them. He annoys them and follows them around, and they, rather like older brothers, tease him and make him play in goal. They let him watch as they play on their playstations and show him what to do. He copies their mannerisms and learns how to say things like 'cool' and 'oh man!' They don't seem to mind if he snuggles up next to them to watch TV. He feels almost as at home in their house as he does in ours and frequently tells me, much to my chagrin, that he prefers Auntie Annie's cooking to mine!

What about my old London friends? Well, predictably, many have fallen by the wayside, although to be fair the process took some time. One friend, who has never contacted me since I left London, was reportedly heard to exclaim that she couldn't possibly keep in touch, because I had everything she wanted and she was far too jealous to continue to be friends with me. Extraordinary, I thought and have scarcely given her another thought since! Some, particularly work colleagues, have simply drifted away; because my life is so different we no longer have much in common. Happily, the ones that really count have continued to be friends. They are a lifeline between my old and new lives and remind me of the person I was before Alan. We now have new friends, too, and I've been dragged through the world of school runs and coffee mornings which, to my astonishment, has turned out to be quite fun.

Naturally, none of this is necessarily exceptional or exclusive to us, as a one-parent family. All extended families rely upon each other to a greater or lesser degree. But in terms of providing a life for Alan, and managing to have a life myself and keep sane, it has been and continues to be essential. Alan and I are a small, rather odd family in the eyes of the world, and these relationships and the support we both gain from them give us a more rounded perspective of the world and help establish our place in it.

I almost forgot to finish the story about the other member of our immediate entourage, Millie the cat: Alan's cat, although you would never know, since she avoids him rather well and rarely appears when he's around. However, the minute Alan is in bed every night, before he is even asleep, Millie turns up and proceeds to harass me throughout the evening. I feed her, I stroke her, I let her settle near me, but this is apparently not enough. She wants to climb on me, and not to just sit, she wants to walk about on me and prod me with her nose every five minutes if I fail to give her my total attention. If I eat anything, she circles me like a jackal. If I'm absorbed in something I'm watching on TV, she contrives to make me jump. It drives me nuts and I am frequently to be heard entreating loudly 'whose idea was it to get a cat?', although it was of course my own idea. Some people I know have dared to suggest that it's not unknown for me to have barmy ideas, which I then act on without properly considering the implications. What a cheek!

3

Would you like another sandwich?

If there's one thing I've learned since I started on the adoption trail, it's that social workers are partial to a good sandwich and a day out! And who can blame them! Theirs is a fairly thankless job. They deserve a treat. Nonetheless, when I first mooted moving out to the sticks, I was initially rather taken aback at how positively the idea was greeted by my largely London-based adoption agency. I was afraid it would be horribly inconvenient for them, given all the traipsing up and down from London they would be required to do. Alan's local authority social workers, too, seemed delighted rather than put out, at the prospect of having to visit me regularly in what must have seemed to them, as "townies", the back of beyond. In the lead-up to legal adoption, it's normal for both the child's social workers and the adopters' social worker to visit on a six-weekly or so basis, just to check how things are going and to give help and advice where needed. I was rather glad of their visits and over the months they became like friends. Alan and I looked forward to seeing them and I think they enjoyed the trip out of "the smoke" as well. And so it transpired that our six-weekly meetings became a rather jolly affair. They nearly always took place on a Friday and, somehow, the social workers always seemed to arrive at around lunchtime! I happily provided lashings of tea and passed round the sandwiches and then we all sat down for a good old chat about my adventures with Alan. It was like something out of Enid Blyton!

*　　*　　*

My family had had mixed feelings about my move back to the country, because they couldn't really see how I'd manage. I convinced them it would be easy initially, whilst I was waiting for a child, to be working in London and living in the country. Many people were doing it already – the early morning London trains from our nearby country town's station were packed every morning with commuters. My parents were reassured and impressed by how much I managed to sell my London flat for (as was I!), and how much I would be able to spend on buying a house closer to them. I remember having a picture in my head of the cottage I would buy for us (me and as yet unknown child) to live in – something straight out of *Country Life* magazine, I rather fancied. And in fact I found the exact thing in the village I grew up in – stone walls, original wooden beams, Aga, a little garden backing on to a protected meadow, almost next door to the church. It was beautiful. Funnily enough, it wasn't until the owners took it off the market that I began to realise how impractical it would have been and that, actually, I'd had a lucky escape. It looked great but it was a) too small and damp, b) too difficult to alter because of the stone walls and conservation regulations (and it didn't have proper central heating) and c) it was simply in the wrong place. For a start, it was in the wrong village. Although this village had been my home when I was young, there was virtually no one left there that I knew. So, when a rather ugly, but much more practical house in the next village came on the market, just yards away from Annie's house and with three bedrooms, big back yard and all mod cons, I was slightly more open to compromise than I might normally have been. I remember having this conversation with my mother (having already seen a picture of the house on the internet):

> Mum: *I went to see the house near Annie's. It's not exactly what you wanted, but I think you should take a look at it.*
>
> Me: *But it looks awful – sort of horrid sixties.*
>
> Mum: *Well, yes it's not a country cottage, but it's got a lot of other things about it. It's got a big garden.*
>
> Me: *Has it?*
>
> Mum: *Yes and it's rather awful inside but it's got great potential.*
>
> Me: *Really?*
>
> Mum: *It's in a very nice street.*
>
> Me: *That's true.*
>
> Mum: *And let's face it, once you're inside and looking out, does it matter what the house you're in looks like? The house opposite looks lovely!*
>
> Me: *Well, yes, that's true. OK, I'll have a look at it.*

* * *

And that was that. A triumph of practicality over frivolity. Well, it had to happen once in my life!

So I moved – out of my London life and into limbo land! My stuff went into storage. I rented a bed-sit in London, quite close to work, where I could stay in the week. At weekends I stayed with my parents, so that I could work on the house. It was a strange life. The tiny bed-sit, with its cupboard-like kitchen and small windows overlooking more small windows and odd bits of rooftop, was cell-like. I could hear noises all the time, but with hardly any view I could never determined what made them or where they came from, which was disconcerting. I never saw any neighbours. I remember thinking at the time, that if I remained single and family-less all my life, I would end up as an old lady in a small apartment like this, perhaps a virtual prisoner in my own home. It was easy to imagine how that could happen. Indeed, I guess it could still happen, since one has no guarantees that one's children will hang around after they've grown and flown the nest.

At the same time as I was juggling living in two places at once, I was working on a TV programme which involved me driving all round the country during the week. It was one of those garden make-over programmes, and I was supervising gardens all over the country. One day I remember getting up at 5am and driving from my home right across to the other side of the country to North Wales to pick up some specially grown plants. I then drove down to St Albans to deliver the plants and then another two hours home to drop off the hired car. I arrived home at about 8pm, after driving pretty much all day. It was exhausting. The whole project was immensely stressful. I was worn out. Eventually, I decided to give up the bed-sit and concentrate on living in one place. I would have to commute, but it seemed as if life would be much simpler. I asked a work friend whether she could tell I was having a difficult time:

> Me: *Did I seem different to you after I'd moved and was living in two places at once?*
>
> Louise: *Well, you coped, but I think you were probably under a lot of stress and I think you were a bit miserable in the evenings in that little bed-sit of yours.*
>
> Me: *Did you think I was mad to do it?*
>
> Louise: *No, I really admired you. You'd thought through*

> *what you felt was wrong with your life and then you found a way to put it right. Once you'd decided what you were going to do you went for it completely. I didn't think you were mad. But it must have taken quite a lot of energy to carry on working the hours you were working and doing all that travelling. Didn't you end up commuting every day?*
>
> Me: *Yes, I couldn't hack living in two places at once.*
>
> Louise: *I think you were completely driven to make the situation work and so you just did it. You probably had some dark times, but you came through.*

* * *

I'm sure that's a very generous assessment of my fading performance at work, but I did come through and I was determined to make a life for myself, and my child, in my new community, which wasn't very easy, given that I was leaving home before 7am every morning and often not getting back again until 10pm. My friendly neighbours introduced themselves and introduced me to other people in the street. Obviously the question arose as to why I'd moved out of London and I decided I would have to be upfront about the adoption, because eventually I would be turning up with a new little boy or girl, and weren't they going to wonder where the child had come from? So I told them, expecting them to think I was a bit strange, and I wasn't disappointed. I could tell from the polite blankness of their expressions that they DID think I was a little strange. I asked my neighbour, Jamie, what her first reaction had been:

> Me: *Didn't you think it was a bit odd that I was going to adopt a child on my own?*
>
> Jamie: *I don't remember thinking that, but I do*

remember wondering how you would manage on your own. I thought about how difficult I found my girls sometimes when Tom (her husband) is away and I wondered if you really knew what you were taking on.

* * *

She thought I was strange alright! Still, I went ahead with the preparations, making some changes to the house and decorating. I chose the room that would be my son/daughter's bedroom and painted it yellow, not having any idea what sex or age my prospective child would be. When I showed curious friends and neighbours around I would say 'And this is the child's room' ... as if it was quite normal for an almost middle-aged single woman to have an empty little child's room in her house!

It had been pointed out to me that when the adoption got the go-ahead, it would all happen very fast, but when I heard that I would be starting to see my new son in one month's time, and that he would be moving in for good in six weeks' time, I was totally unprepared. I rushed around frantically trying to finish off jobs in the house and buying necessary equipment. My Mum, caught up in the excitement too, helped me find a buggy, bought clothes and so on. I told the neighbours, who were politely amazed. I tried to make the little bedroom seem homely for my new little boy. I left work, breathing a huge sigh of relief as I walked out of the door for the final time. I felt as if I was walking out of my old life and heading straight for the new one. It was all I could do not to run!

My new life was to be a family life – that was the intention. Yet, even after five years of living here, Alan and I are often not included in other people's family events or weekend parties. In fact, these other people discuss these family-oriented occasions in front of me, the whys and wherefores of whether or not they were invited, for instance, and it never seems to occur to them that we weren't invited or included and that we might mind. To be honest, most of the time I don't mind, and Annie and I sometimes have a giggle about the appalling, but rather hilarious, lack of sensitivity in some of these conversations. Weekends are probably the most lonely times, because, without the school run, and the chats in the playground of a morning, I sometimes don't get to talk to another adult for two whole days. My parents bear the brunt of this, as Alan and I often "drop in" at weekends. In theory we're just passing, but truthfully, it's also because I crave a face-to-face conversation with another grown-up. And the loneliness hasn't come as a total surprise – for one thing, it's an extension of being single without children, which is something I'm very used to. Some very "couply" groups find single females hard to deal with. I've often heard stories of women, in particular, who unexpectedly find themselves alone in the world, after a divorce, or even after a bereavement, because their social lives suddenly take a dive. I had been warned by other single adopters that life might be like this and I was prepared for a degree of isolation. Being prepared, though, doesn't mean it doesn't sometimes hurt, and part of me wishes things could be different; like many harassed mothers, I have a rich fantasy life and occasionally I have this day-dream:

> *My tall dark husband and I (me dressed in something floral but tasteful) bundle a cheerful Alan in the back of the Range Rover, together with a cold box full of beer and cleverly home-made somethings and we roll up to one of our friends' houses, where my husband cracks jokes with cricket references, at which all of the women roll their eyes conspiratorially and all the men laugh. Alan quickly joins in playing with all the other perfect little children, who are delighted to see him, and he plays nicely, without hitting or name calling, until required to come and eat something, at which point he*

delicately consumes a couple of sausages and something healthy from the variety of delightful home-made salads on offer. He doesn't wipe his mouth on his T-shirt or completely ignore me, or say that he hates salad and the sausages tasted horrible. But if he did answer back with something verging on an unsuitable tone of voice, my husband would firmly, but discreetly, admonish him (something like 'don't talk to your mother like that, old man!') and they would smile at each other, knowing that my well-being was safe in their caring hands.

Yeah, right!

* * *

Why have I included this little story in a chapter about moving? Well, partly because none of this would have been an issue if we'd stayed in the city. My single status would not have been important either socially or at Alan's school. But in our little village, we are a rather rare breed – I can only think of maybe half a dozen other children here who are without a live-in father. However, that's insignificant in the face of the many advantages of life in the country: the security of living in a small village community, for instance, is something that will help Alan in the long term. He feels safe, which is so important to him, given how unsafe he must have felt at the beginning of his life. While some may find the village telegraph and the "everyone knows everyone's business" thing annoying, I find it predictable and, well, comforting actually. I frankly don't have the time or energy to do anything particularly outrageous, so I haven't figured much on the grapevine so far (at least, I don't think so, anyway!). One funny incident concerning my "status" happened when I first started taking Alan to the local toddler group. A rather prolific gossip, well known for her mischievous tongue, approached me:

> *Gossip: Do you have a partner, Julia, because I've seen a lady out the front of your house doing*

> *gardening and I wondered...*
>
> Me: *(sniggering) Oh... Yes, that's my mother. She likes to help out sometimes.*
>
> Gossip: *Oh, I see! I thought maybe...*
>
> Me: *No, there's just me and Alan.*

* * *

Nowadays, my single-ness is old news as far as the gossip-mongers are concerned.

So what are the other benefits of our country life? Mostly, space and familiarity. When we go out, we see people we know all the time. Alan doesn't feel anonymous, or that he doesn't count. He feels known and likes to chat to neighbours and their dogs and cats. We have enough room to grow things and, particularly when Alan was small, we had a big vegetable patch, which he helped his new Grandad to look after. It was the perfect way for him to spend time with an adult male and was the beginning of his great relationship with his Grandad. I bought Alan a climbing frame with a slide, because he loves to climb and he has space in the garden to play football, to run about and generally to let off steam when he needs to (or when I need him to). He learned to ride his bike on the patio. He chats to the kids next door and plays with them. He shouts and waves at his friends as they pass by. We can walk to the shops, or round the corner to Annie's house. It's a good childhood, one that would not have been possible in London. In fact, I realise, it's very much like my own childhood was and, of course, that's not really an accident. It's something of me that I can give to Alan, which will hopefully help him throughout his life; this sense of belonging and knowing that he can be safe. We are part of the community, so while we may have to put up with the gossipmongers, they're our gossip-mongers and besides, we get to gossip about them too, so there!

Talking about sandwiches, which is how I began this

chapter, I'm led towards another issue of a slightly personal nature. I am, to use a phrase coined by a popular novelist of our time, "traditionally built". That is to say that I am slightly, no... rather more than slightly, overweight. I think I'm probably ever so slightly more overweight now than I was when I first took the adoption road. But let's just say that when I presented myself at the beginning of the process I was larger than average. Apparently, some adoption agencies frown on this and have rules about it. Fat equals unfit, in more ways than one, they say. However, I was fortunate to be in the hands of a rather more enlightened agency. They assessed my general health. It was good. They looked at my attitudes and were happy. They saw what I'd achieved in life both personally and in terms of work and figured I was a reasonable bet. Hoorah for them! Alan's social worker was also fine with it. Alan's birth mum was of a generous build, his foster mum was more than ample so, from Alan's point of view, I filled the bill. In fact, no one's really made an issue of it at all. Occasionally, less and less now since I've known all of Alan's classmates from when they were small and I'm now mostly invisible to them, Alan and I have this sort of conversation:

Me: *Why did you hit Gerry?*

Alan: *Gerry said you were fat.*

Me: *I am fat.*

Alan: *I know but I didn't like Gerry saying that.*

Me: *Well, I don't care what Gerry thinks. Anyway, he probably only said it to upset you, so the best thing to do is to try not to get upset and then he won't say it any more.*

Alan: *I'm gonna hit him again.*

Me: *That won't help. You'll hurt him and you'll just get yourself in trouble. I'll tell you what, if he says it again. Just say 'yes, she is fat, so what?'. OK?*

Alan: *OK... (doubtful).*

> *Me:*   *He thinks he's being clever but he's only saying something that any silly billy can see – that I'm a bit fat. It's like saying (using silly whiny voice) 'you've got blonde hair and blue eyes'! It would be true but it wouldn't be a very clever thing to say, would it?*
>
> *Alan:*   *(laughing) No!*

*   *   *

I admit, I've tried losing weight, but it's a difficult time for dieting. I'm on my own a lot in the evenings and, let's face it, being a mother is very much like being a social worker on a small scale, in that it doesn't seem to matter what you do, someone will tell you it isn't right! It would be enough to drive even the most restrained compulsive eater straight into the fridge. As it is, I rather miss my Friday lunches with Alan's social workers. Like them, I think I deserve the odd treat. Would I like another sandwich (low carb, low fat on wholemeal with salad)? Yes, please!

4

How I committed financial suicide and survived

I've never really been a financial success and I've always rather hoped that I would meet a handsome millionaire some day. Of course I know that won't happen and some people might say that I was incredibly foolish deliberately to chuck in an extremely well-paid job without much of an idea of how I would manage financially in the future – especially as I was going to be responsible for another little person's well-being. All I can say in my defence is that the highly paid work didn't make me happy, but that the idea of being a mother really did; and as most people seem to manage somehow without pots of cash, I figured I could too, even though I wasn't quite sure how in the first instance. Those who know me well sat back to watch with interest, to see how one such as I, with a reputation for extravagance, would cope. There had been various situations in the past when I had displayed a tendency to spend apparently recklessly when thrift would have been the wisest path. Many years ago, for example, when I was between jobs, I remember my friend Annie laughing at me because although I was very, very hard up, I splashed out on an expensive jar of French mustard. I reminded her about that recently:

> Me: *You remember the French mustard incident? Did you think I would be able to cope with being poor this time?*
>
> Annie: *I thought you would find it hard.*
>
> Me: *As I explained to you at the time – having French mustard transformed a very cheap luncheon meat sandwich into something slightly exotic. It made me feel better about being poor.*
>
> Annie: *I don't suppose it's worth me saying you could have had a ham sandwich instead of luncheon meat if you hadn't bought the mustard?*
>
> Me: *Yes, but the mustard lasted a long time, so according to my calculations I could eventually have ham AND mustard, which would feel even more luxurious. It was a lot less depressing somehow.*
>
> Annie: *I guess I never realised how much of a morale booster French mustard was!*

* * *

Ever since, French mustard has stood as a symbol for me of my attempts to stay sane when my bank account is dwindling. 'You can't make an omelette without breaking eggs'; 'there's no gain without pain'; 'you have to speculate to accumulate' – these are all maxims I have internalised over the years, possibly, some would say, to justify my financial recklessness. I confess, I've made a number of "money-saving" investments in the past and they represent the sort of extravagance that's ammunition for my critics. This time, I don't think I disappointed them on any front for once again, the first "economies" I made typically involved me spending lots of money (much secret shaking of heads must have gone on and lots of knowing looks been exchanged), but despite behaviour which may have appeared impulsive and financially dangerous, most of it was the result of planning and a huge amount of thinking – in other words, there was method in my apparent madness. One person who understood my rationale is my mother (I guess that explains where I got it from!):

> Me: *Did you think I was being rash with money when I started spending – for instance on the new car?*
>
> Mum: *Not really, no. I could see what you were doing. You'd had no end of trouble with old cars, I could understand the need for a reliable car that probably wouldn't break down and would save you money in repairs. I could see you would have plenty to worry about, without having to spend any time worrying about your car.*
>
> Me: *So you didn't feel that I hadn't thought it through?*
>
> Mum: *Oh no, I could see that you were preparing for a different life. I'd have done exactly the same thing.*

* * *

My first extravagance, of course, was the house. My flat in London sold for a ridiculous amount of money, which meant that I could completely get rid of my mortgage. I suppose I could have gone on to buy a modest abode with just two bedrooms and a small garden, but I wanted space if I was going to stay at home a lot with my new son/daughter. I wanted him or her to have plenty of room to play. Furthermore, I suppose I could have simply saved what was left over of the money, but instead I made some changes to the house and garden and had everywhere decorated – well, it really did need it. The previous owners had several big dogs and the house reeked of dog. Every room was dark and neglected. Actually, I told myself, the house was cheap for its size so I was justified in spending money on making it sanitary! My next extravagance was the aforementioned new car. I needed it immediately, because when I first moved house I was travelling up and down to London in an old brown Montego, given to me by a friend. It broke down regularly on the M25. Many is the morning I've spent on the hard shoulder, trying to make myself heard on my mobile phone as I explained to my boss why, once again, I would be late for work. The new car, all shiny and clean, was guaranteed for three years and I knew I wouldn't have to worry about MOTs for three years either – so three years of financial peace of mind regarding the car. As my astute mother quite rightly pointed out, I already had enough to worry about without putting up with a dodgy car.

My next purchase, and I like to think of it as my pièce de résistance, cost several hundred pounds, and probably perplexed even my understanding mother at first. I bought a tent! Yes, it was expensive, but boy has it been worth it! Initially, my critics were dumbfounded, but I like to view it as a triumph of forward planning, particularly as I spent an uncharacteristic amount of time researching the tent, which has been paramount in its success as part of our lives. Let me explain. I felt it would be important for my child and me to go away on holiday at least once a year – I wanted him to have something to talk about at the end of the school holidays and I wanted him or her to see more of the world than just our little village. I felt I would need to get away for short breaks too. Camping would be cheap and would feel like an adventure, or so I hoped.

I looked around at tents of all sorts of shapes and sizes and it occurred to me that the most important thing was that I should be able to erect it on my own, with a little help from my child. Fortunately, I found one I could manage, although I have on several occasions been partially airborne, owing to sudden gusts of wind, and sailed kite-like across a campsite, waving wildly to Alan, shouting at him to grab on to the nearest tent pole. Were it not for other friendly helpful campers, there are times when Alan and I may quite easily have found ourselves floating across the north sea, next stop Norway, which would have been slightly more adventurous than I was planning. But mostly, with maybe a little bit of help from new friends, I can put the thing up solo.

The next important consideration on the tent list was what would happen if it rained a lot. Could I cope with grovelling around on my knees all day? Answer – no, I couldn't. So I had to find a tent in which I could stand up, move around, fit a table inside and so on. As camping in the UK involves much wet weather strategy I feel vindicated for the extra cost of a tent which was large enough for us to go on living inside during rainstorms without me developing a permanent stoop!

The final feature of our tent concerned the sleeping arrangements. While my child, when small, and I would want to share a sleeping compartment, I thought it would be nice to make it possible to take friends with us. Therefore, I looked around at four-man tents, many of which had sleeping compartments in close quarters. Fine for close family, but with friends, I decided slightly more distance might be appreciated.

Eventually, I found the perfect tent – hang the cost – with a tall square area in the middle, tall enough for standing up and big enough for a table and chairs, and with two sleeping compartments, one at either end. I spent a little more money on various pieces of basic equipment, but saved on sleeping paraphernalia since we take our duvets and lots of pillows to help us sleep comfortably in our home away from home. Sometimes we take friends, and sometimes we go alone. But all in all, we have had numerous wonderful camping trips, when we have paid approximately £10 per night to stay close to the beach or close to friends: almost cheaper than staying at home. Honest!

Though I may have appeared extravagant, I managed in most areas to create a basis for a sustainable lifestyle. So if my plans thus far all seem rather whimsical, I should point out that I also thought very much about how everyday life could work if I couldn't go out and earn money. After all, there seemed no point in going to all this trouble to have a child, and then handing him or her over to a child-minder or a nanny, while I went off to work everyday. I figured a child that may have had much upheaval already in its short life deserved at the very least a mummy who would stick around. Clearly, the key to financial harmony is savings, and if I'd had some, life would have been much less of a headache, so I would urge any prospective single adopter to start saving immediately. As it was, I had a few savings accounts, each containing approximately 38p, but I gamely started buying savings stamps as a last minute attempt, and was astonished at what was available – TV licence stamps, car tax stamps – it's definitely worth investigating. I also save supermarket vouchers like mad and I have needed to rely on stamps and vouchers when things have been particularly difficult. Just recently, now that my car is getting older and may soon require attention, I used my supermarket vouchers to join the RAC. Who says you can't get something for nothing!

So, how did I imagine I was going to be able to support myself and child in the future? Well, having bought a three-bedroomed house, I converted one room into what I grandly named my "office" and explained to my concerned parents that this would be useful for "working from home", although I don't think I fooled them for a minute; I had no idea what WORK I would be doing!

However, something I discovered during a pre-approval weekend workshop at my adoption agency helped enormously, and it's important information, particularly for single adopters without a second income. The subject of adoption leave came up during a discussion about financial arrangements and it was the first I'd ever heard of such a thing. During that same weekend it was stressed that if a suitable child became available for us immediately, or at any time before approval, the approval process could be fast-tracked. In other words, said the presiding social worker (sandwiches at my house were as yet not even a glimmer in her eye), you need to start talking to people about your plans, especially if you may need to leave work rather suddenly and you should enquire what sort of adoption leave, if any, is offered by your company. Actually, it was to take another year and a half before I would need to leave work suddenly, but as a result of these words of advice, I completely panicked, decided to bite the bullet and let my work know what I was doing.

First thing on the following Monday morning I made an appointment to see my Personnel Officer, so that I could find out if they had any sort of adoption leave provisions – the terms of it varied from company to company, I'd been told, and I wanted to find out what I could count on.

My downtrodden Personnel Officer looked somewhat startled at the beginning of our interview. I had been deliberately obscure about the purpose of it. I imagine she was expecting some kind of confrontation – a complaint or an unreasonable request of some sort – so when I started babbling on about adoption and maternity leave she visibly relaxed and was clearly so grateful that I wasn't going to break down and cry about bullying in the workplace, or sexual harassment, that she couldn't do enough to help me out! And the news was very good. My company had a very progressive attitude to adoption leave, it seemed, although no one in my Personnel Officer's living memory had ever taken advantage of it. She looked it up in an enormous book of rules. I nearly asked her to keep on looking in case there was anything else I might be entitled to claim! Anyway, it turned out that I would be offered the exact equivalent of my firm's maternity leave arrangements – 18 weeks paid leave and 11 weeks unpaid leave, although the unpaid leave would depend on a recommendation from my adoption agency that it was necessary – which of course it would be. The only difference between maternity leave and adoption leave as far as I could tell was that adoption leave could be taken suddenly, with a minimal amount of prior warning. I was thrilled, for although I had been fairly gung ho about my finances, deep down I had been worried that I was committing financial suicide from which I wouldn't recover.

At the same time as I resolved to talk to my Personnel Officer, I decided to let my boss into the secret, just in case I needed to leave in a hurry. I dreaded having to talk to him, because he was the sort of hard-nosed journalist (and a man) who, I believed, would not understand for a moment why I would want to adopt and leave a job he felt most people would give their right arm for. So I marched into his office one morning in a most confrontational manner and closed the door, sat down with great purpose and, before he had a chance to say anything, blurted out the whole story. He sat and listened quietly, his face totally inscrutable and I wasn't even sure that he was listening, until I reached the end of my monologue and paused for breath. He smiled and we went on to have this conversation:

> Me: *So what do you think?*
> Ian: *Well...*

Me:	(slightly alarmed by his composure) Of course, I'll try to let you have as much notice as possible…
Ian:	That's not important, but listen, you're not going to believe this, but my wife and I are in exactly the same boat as you at the moment. We have two daughters, but my wife would like a son and so we've decided to adopt a little boy.
Me:	Oh! Wow…
Ian:	Of course, I'd be grateful if you'd keep it to yourself, and don't worry, I won't tell anyone what you've told me…
Me:	Of course, thanks…
Ian:	I know exactly what you're going through, so you take as much time as you like – if you need to take time off for meetings or workshops, just let me know. And best of luck, really.
Me:	Well thank you, and the same to you. Thanks…

* * *

I was shocked. Well, I was expecting to be patronised, not congratulated, which just goes to show how wrong you can be. I was glad all round that I hadn't kept things to myself, because if you're going to plan effectively you need to know what you're up against and people are not going to be on your side if they don't know there's a side to be on!

Obviously, when the adoption leave expired and the money dried up, I would have to start thinking about what to do next, but the breathing space would allow me to carry on planning.

Once I was based in the country, with a small child, it became fairly clear that I wouldn't be returning to my time-consuming job in London. While I was contemplating this, and trying to keep in touch with the word on the street at work, I heard through the grapevine that in some departments (not mine, as it happened) my company was seeking voluntary redundancies. I quickly contacted my obliging Personnel Officer and asked if the company would consider me for redundancy, even though they weren't specifically looking in my direction. Happily, they agreed and the settlement gave me yet more breathing space. In fact, it was a whole year before I needed to look for work to support us.

There is no doubt that with only one person bringing home the bacon, the pressure can be intense. There have been times over the years when money has been very short, both before I worked and while working, because there are always expenses with children that you don't anticipate. For instance, you can't anticipate that a child will cut up a perfectly good pair of trousers with scissors, just to see what happens; you can't guess (well I couldn't then, at least) how quickly they will wear out their shoes or grow out of their clothes, or that things in the house will break down and how much it will cost to repair them.

Since we started out, I have been obliged to take out a small mortgage, which has helped me to maintain a reasonable lifestyle, but despite this, there have been weeks, normally towards the end of the month, when we have lived entirely off Alan's child benefit, which amounts to less than £20 per week. These weeks have involved a lot of shopping around, which is time consuming, a lot more cooking from scratch, which I'm not particularly good at, but amazingly, when you have to, the impossible can be done. Sometimes we eat the same thing several times in a week, which frankly Alan loves, because he has a fairly limited repertoire of foods he "likes" anyway. I have found all sorts of value stores, which sell everyday foods and other household necessities more cheaply than the major supermarkets, and I try not to worry about where they come from or how much the people producing them are paid. I have occasionally drawn the line – for example, in our local cheap store one week they were selling frozen chickens at a ridiculous knock-down price, but the packaging, including sell-by date and cooking instructions, was only in Russian. Perhaps I overreacted, but I did feel that was maybe just a step too far!

* * *

It is now five years down the line and, although I undoubtedly have earning power, I'm feeling the pinch quite badly. I've accepted we will never be rich, because I am unwilling to sacrifice this important time with Alan. But we scrape by, sometimes well and sometimes not quite so well. Soon it will be Christmas and Alan has started his yearly 'I want' crescendo towards Christmas Eve. At the weekend he spent a long time looking through the Argos catalogue, ticking off something on every page that he REALLY wanted. I worked out it would cost me somewhere in the region of £10,000 to provide everything on his list! Much as I would love to give him everything he wants so Alan will not feel too hard done by, it won't happen and I think most families face this same dilemma every year, on some level or another, regardless of how much money they have to spend. We won't be giving lots of gifts this year, but we will have a wonderful, loving family Christmas. Alan will get something he really wants and I don't really want anything much. It's enough for me that we are a happy family, that we are (more or less) independent and have a lifestyle that we can just about sustain and that sustains us.

My planning, haphazard though it may have appeared from the outside, helped enormously and I think that I have proved there is life after financial suicide, although we exist on a slightly different socio-economic level from the one I leapt off to become a single adopter. But I survived and I think I may have even managed to impress some of my doubting friends. For instance, Annie was so impressed by the success of my tent extravagance, that she too bought a tent. Unfortunately, she didn't do her research, she cut corners and bought a cheap one. We all went to Dorset for a week and when the rain came, well, she got a bit wet! Funnily enough, when I offered her some French mustard with her bangers and mash, she didn't have a thing to say!

5

Becoming "Mummy"

The first day I met Alan I was sort of in shock, really, and feeling naturally terribly nervous. I knew a lot about Alan and I'd seen some pictures of him. He'd heard of me too. I'd made him a little book about myself, my family and my home, and I knew that his foster mother, whom Alan called Nanny, had been going through the book with him. In the book I'd written 'Hello, my name is Julia,' but Nanny, who knew better, had apparently been saying to him 'Look, Alan, that's Mummy'. Now, Alan had never really called anyone else Mummy. He'd had regular contact with his birth mother, but she didn't figure much in his life. He knew other children had mummies, because his friends at nursery school had mummies who came to collect them at the end of each session. How was he to know what mummies were and how was he to know they didn't just turn up one day out of the blue and claim their little boys, just as I was about to?

When I arrived at the foster family's home, I trembled as I knocked on the door. Nanny opened it, we said hello and then suddenly there was little Alan, bright as a button and very excited. 'Who's this?' Nanny asked. 'It's

Mummy,' cried Alan.

*   *   *

I suppose I was in my mid-thirties when I discovered that it would be very difficult for me to have children. It was after I'd been ill and I remember being a little shaken by the news, but I would have to admit that not being with a partner meant there was no pressure to have babies, and not having ever had a strong maternal urge, I was not too unhappy about it. I guess I had never really given myself time to think through having babies or being a family. My parents knew I couldn't have babies. They never mentioned it. If they were sad about not having grandchildren, they didn't say so.

As I began to reflect on what my life was about and what it was going to be about in the future, and having tried other avenues to give my life meaning, it was with a sense of recognition that I realised I wanted to have my own family and that I wanted to be a mother, if I could. I thought about trying to get pregnant and even bought some books about it, but going through all manner of painful and expensive medical procedures to try and have a child on my own seemed both fraught with problems and incredibly self-centred. I was forty – did I really want to be pregnant on my own at my age? No, I didn't.

I tried to envisage myself as a mother – I looked around at other mothers I knew. It looked easy. 'I can do that,' I thought. I watched what went on, chatted to my friends with children, spent time with my friends' children. I really felt I could do it. It didn't seem like rocket science.

It wasn't until I'd already pretty much made up my mind about adopting that I decided to discuss it with anyone. People were used to me being on my own and being a career-centred person. I wondered whether they would be able to make the transition to seeing me as a mummy sort of a person or whether they would see this as just another hobby – a fad that would pass. Would they think I was suitable or simply mad and wilful? I wondered if all prospective single adopters had the same feeling about changing roles:

> Me: *Do you think people felt that adoption was just something you latched onto – another "project"?*
>
> Carol: *Yes I think some did – probably the ones who didn't know me as well as they thought!*
>
> Me: *Did you have any worries about your friends accepting you in your new role?*
>
> Carol: *Not really. I think I assumed some friends would just drift out of my life, as they do whenever your life changes or you move house or whatever. I've watched a lot of my friends become parents the "normal" way. I don't think it was that different for me, except that my new "baby" wasn't a baby and could speak for himself, so they were instantly required to start developing a relationship with him too.*

* * *

I was forgetting, of course, that my friends hadn't always been mummies either. I tried to remember my friends before they were parents. It was difficult to recall how they were. It never occurred to me that they wouldn't cope as parents. But what did I know then? I asked Annie whether she found the thought of me being a mummy at all disturbing:

> Me: *Didn't it seem to you like an odd idea – me becoming a mum?*
>
> Annie: *Well, only because you weren't one at the time. It was hard to imagine you in a different role. I didn't think you COULDN'T be a mum.*
>
> Me: *I suppose it's always a bit like that when someone has their first baby.*
>
> Annie: *Yes it is. People have to adjust. When you're*

pregnant, though, people have quite a long time to adjust, you have longer yourself to get used to the idea, and the pregnancy kind of forces the change.

Me: *That's true. With me it was more, one day I wasn't a mum and the next day I was!*

Annie: *I suppose I was more concerned about you being a mummy without a daddy.*

Me: *Ah, yes. That little thing.*

Annie: *I thought you'd make a good mum, though.*

Me: *Thanks. Question is, were you right?*

Annie: *Don't be daft!*

* * *

I didn't have a pregnancy to cope with, but I did have a very long time to think about being a mum. It took two years from the time I decided to go ahead to the time when I first met Alan and took him home. My life changed in many ways during that period – moving house, commuting – outside of work my life was substantially different. To my co-workers and my friends in London, though, I must have seemed largely the same old me and I'm sure I carried on in the same old way. Getting ready to be a mother was rather like being involved in some long-term project with no particular deadline – in some ways it didn't seem as if it would ever happen.

During this lengthy build-up, I do recall having "mummy fantasies", about what it would be like to have a little person around. I could sort of envisage a life with another little person in it – after all, I'd got a room in my new house that I'd decorated for him or her. Meanwhile, when *Be My Parent* arrived each month, I scanned the pictures, feeling terrible for all the children, and hoping for some divine inspiration. When I first started chatting through things with my social worker, Sam, I just assumed that I would adopt a little girl. We had this conversation:

Sam: *Have you thought about whether you'd prefer to have a girl or a boy?*

Me: *Yes, well I'd like a girl of course.*

Sam: *Why of course?*

Me: *I don't know really. I suppose because I feel as if I don't know anything about boys...and I'll be on my own. There won't be a male around. I just imagined it would be easier all round if I had a girl.*

Sam: *You know, it's funny, but I've always imagined you with a little boy.*

Me: *Really? Why's that?*

Sam: *I'm not sure, exactly. I just can see you with a little boy.*

Me: *Oh! Well, I hadn't really thought about having a boy. I suppose there's no harm in thinking about it.*

*   *   *

And so I did. I thought it through and decided it was more important to find the right child, regardless of whether they were a boy or girl and then, as it happened, I spotted Alan. To this day, I'm not sure what attracted me to him. The description in *Be My Parent* was frank about his background – I read that both his parents had mental illnesses, which could have implications for him in the future. I think the main point was that Alan was a healthy, normal little boy right now, and I felt I could handle that. Also, his birthday was on the same day as my Mum's, which I felt was a bit of an omen. It also mentioned him splashing around in the sea on holiday, which conjured up such a cute picture that I couldn't help myself. My friends who've had children the normal way have often spoken about how, when they first saw their newborn babies, they kind of fell in love. Something about that chubby little face called out to me. I don't know how or why, but I knew

Alan was destined to be my son the minute I clapped eyes on him!

It was agreed that I would spend two weeks after our first meeting seeing Alan every day, before I was to take him home. So I spent two weeks hanging out with him and taking him out on little trips. The first time I took him out on my own we went to a nearby playground and then to McDonalds. He was such a scruffy little urchin – he didn't look very healthy – too many sweets and McDonalds, I suspect. It was odd to be in charge of this little stranger, who kept calling me mummy. I felt more like an auntie, in fact. The next time I took him out, we went to Richmond Park to see the ducks. He loved them – still does, actually – I remember being terrified that he would run off. The third time we went out together, we went to London Zoo. It was amusing how, and now I know this to be typical of Alan, he was more interested in the sparrows that kept flying in and out of the hedges than he was in the lions and tigers. I remember him pointing to a little pond and shouting out with delight, 'Mummy, look at the waw'er' in his really strong London accent, and thinking to myself, how on earth will this little person and I ever fit together as a family? It seems so strange to recall those feelings, now that Alan and I are firmly bonded and most definitely a family.

Finally, it was time for me to whisk my new son away from everything he knew and take him home with me for good. I had previously warned the neighbours, and my friends and my Mum were positively champing at the bit to see him. I was so proud of this lovely boy who was now mine that I couldn't wait to show him off, but I was nervous about how I would be. Would I just start being a mummy? How would that work?

Hearing me being called mummy was at first quite a laugh for my friends, I think. I was aware of nudges and giggles each time Alan said it:

> Me: Come on, be honest, it was weird hearing Alan call me mummy, wasn't it?
>
> Annie: Well, it was a bit. It just took a little getting used to, that's all. We soon did get used to it.
>
> Me: It took me a while, actually.
>
> Annie: I know. I suppose I'd been a mummy for quite some time already before my children actually were able to say mummy. It was nice, though. I liked hearing Alan call you mummy.

* * *

For my parents, I think hearing Alan call me mummy was very moving, but of course they were also grappling with being Grandma and Grandad for the first time!

Several months after Alan came to live with me, I took him to London and we visited my old office. It was much more of a shock to my former work colleagues, I think, to see me in this unfamiliar role, particularly for those of them who hadn't quite believed I would go through with it. They thought Alan was adorable, naturally, but it was as if I had grown horns or changed colour or something. I had by then become accustomed to being a mummy, and all that it entailed, but they found it hard to see what I had already realised, which is that I hadn't actually changed at all. I was still me – same sense of humour, same personality – but now I had a little extra something – Alan – who had become the centre of my universe, and work just wasn't that interesting to me any more.

My new friends, the ones I met through toddler groups and pre-school, just accepted I was a mum because they hadn't known me in any other context. My old close friends soon got used to it. Even I got used to being a mummy much more quickly than I had imagined. For Alan, though, it was a slightly more complicated process. Alan knew that I was Mummy – that was my name – but although he knew other children had mummies he didn't really know what a mummy was for. For many months after Alan first came to live with me, I really had the impression that he didn't understand that we belonged together in a family unit. If we were out with other adults, even in an environment where he didn't know anyone else, I would often get the distinct feeling that he would have been happy to go home with anyone who asked him. He was happy to accept attention and hugs from any adult prepared to give them, particularly men. It worried me enormously, because Alan had absolutely no fear or reticence with adult strangers. Even now, several years later, I sometimes have to talk to him about being familiar with adults that he doesn't know. It would take months before I really felt, when we were out and about, that Alan knew he was supposed to be with me, and that he had to come home with me, and that he was happy about it.

In time, clues to Alan's attachment to me started to appear – for instance, if I ever left him with anyone, which wasn't often, he would start to ask where I was after a certain amount of time. Having been very compliant in his first few months with me, he started to be rather naughty and angry with me, which I took to be a sign that he felt secure enough to risk upsetting me. If he fell and hurt himself, instead of trying hard not to show that he was hurt, he would cry and come and find me. I had always tried to be affectionate and physically close to him, which helped the bonding process enormously. We hugged a lot – we still do. He is a very cuddly child.

The "daddy" thing has always been and continues to be an issue. We are happy and our family works well, but with hindsight, I would have to be honest and say that if I'd been part of a couple, the establishment of our family and Alan's ability to feel secure within it, would probably have happened more easily. My position as mummy would most definitely have been easier to define because, as it is, I have to provide all the parenting myself – both the nurturing and the discipline, kind of simultaneously, which does lead to a certain amount of confusion and adds to my parental angst. However, life is never straightforward and my friends constantly remind me that couples don't necessarily do the job better. Divorce and bad marriages affect kids in terrible ways and I would certainly not want Alan to be subjected to those kinds of traumas on top of what he's already been through.

*   *   *

So, at our very first meeting, Alan came running to the door of Nanny's house and recognised me from the pictures he'd seen. I was astonished at this bright little chap who knew I was his mummy. When I remember that moment, in my head it's like one of those romantic wedding pictures that you see, where the couple are in the centre of the picture and they're framed by a sort of blurry line that suggests the mists of time or whatever. The truth is that he came running to the door, with a bottle of sugary drink dripping all over him. He had something horrible and sticky all round his mouth and his nappy, a frankly rather stinky one, was hanging off him. Somehow, although it must have registered somewhere in my memory, I didn't notice that at the time. Love at first sight? Yes, I think so.

6

I won't be coming in today

No job is ideal and when you first start working somewhere there are always clues to what might go wrong. When I began my career as a working mum, however, I was so impressed with myself that I noticed nothing. I even remained oblivious when the very-pleasant-to-your-face-if-rather-condescending office manager, Jennifer, tried to explain in my original interview how my prospective boss liked to work. She said *'You've got a four-year-old son haven't you? You must understand about tantrums and foot stamping. Well, you should be able to manage Graham quite well!'* We both laughed. Well you would, wouldn't you? That was before I knew better. I was suffering from temporary blindness having been rendered insensible by the words "Holiday Play Scheme", a subsidised and well-managed childcare arrangement that ran during all the school holidays. Fantastic, I thought. The answer to all my problems. Silly me! Nothing is that easy and nothing comes without a price.

* * *

I hadn't thought through what would happen if Alan was ill, because actually he hardly ever is. When it first happened, I thought 'no cause for alarm, I'll just ring up work and take the day off':

Conversation 1 (When I haven't been in the new job very long)

> Work: *(Ring ring…) Hello?*
>
> Me: *Oh hi! It's Julia Wise here.*
>
> Work: *Hi Julia.*
>
> Me: *Look, I'm really sorry, but my son has chicken pox. I won't be coming in today – well probably not all week actually…*
>
> Work: *Oh dear. Poor Alan. I'll let the office manager know. Is he really itchy?*
>
> Me: *Yes, he's feeling very uncomfortable at the moment.*
>
> Work: *Poor him and poor you. Have you had it?*
>
> Me: *Yes, fortunately. Look I'm sorry to let people down, but I'll definitely be in at the beginning of next week. Could you let Graham know too? If he has any problems with anything, he can always give me a call at home.*
>
> Work: *Listen, don't worry about it. I'll tell him. I hope Alan feels better soon. Bye.*
>
> Me: *Thanks very much. Bye.*

* * *

There – that sounds lovely and understanding, doesn't it? Shame it didn't last.

Looking at it from my employers' point of view, you can see how absence because of a child's sickness would start to get on their nerves. But that's the problem with being a working mum – and this is the same whether you're single or with a partner – however much you manage to sort out your hours to fit in with the school run, and organise some kind of official or unofficial childcare in case of emergencies, you can't stop your child from being ill and you simply can't farm them out to strangers, or even family, if they're poorly. As a single parent, you're stuck with being the only one available to juggle (although, I observe there aren't many women who can count on their husbands to stay at home if the kids are sick). It doesn't matter how understanding they are at your workplace, it doesn't take long for the work-life balance to kick in – and your employers' idea of work-life balance regarding you is, I've discovered, the exact inverse of your own! So whilst I was entitled to take time off when Alan was ill, this company I worked for would make me use my holidays to cover it, so by the time it came around to the actual holidays, my potential days off had dwindled to almost nothing! There is a sneaky way round this, and that is when your children are ill you call up and pretend YOU are ill and take sick leave so that it doesn't affect your holiday entitlement – not something I was ever tempted to do, naturally, but the system kind of encourages that sort of behaviour, if you know what I mean.

Before Alan, I was a workaholic. I don't think my bosses thought of me that way, because, hey, occasionally I went home and sometimes I took all weekend off; and I always got the feeling that it didn't matter how much I worked, it was never enough for them! The television industry is a little bit like that – and is exempt, by the way, from regulations concerning the number of hours you can work without a break. Now, I know women who work in TV and who hardly ever seem to be at home. It's a choice. They want the lifestyle and the money and they have a nanny – sometimes two nannies! But the truth is, I was a little jealous of my friends who'd done the whole Mummy thing – afternoon walks, toddler groups, coffee mornings and so on.

So when at last it became obvious that I would have to

work for a living again, I began to look around for something I could do at home – remember my redundant "office"? By this time, Alan was attending pre-school nursery and I was deeply involved in the pre-school committee. I decided to ask around and discovered that the mother of one of Alan's friends had a telephone sales job she did from home. To my delight the company were hiring. This mother explained the Working Family Tax Credit to me (now Working Tax Credit) and said that the company she worked for would be happy to register me for the 16 hours a week needed to qualify for Tax Credit. So I would earn money from the job – which involved telephoning and using my computer – and my salary would be made up to a certain level by the Tax Credit. Hoorah! At last my "office" would come into its own.

I discussed my situation with the company and they agreed that although the job was for term-time only, they would be happy to spread my pay out over the year and I would be paid monthly. Illness was not a problem, because I could still just about work if Alan was home and I was rarely so ill that I couldn't prop myself up in front of the computer or croak down the phone.

During the holidays, I was able to be with Alan, so childcare was not a problem either. In fact it worked marvellously for a whole year. Perfect, you might think! Well, yes, but... the job was DEATHLY boring. It consisted of telephoning schools – lots and lots of them on a big long list – and trying to sell them a computer course for their Teaching Assistants. It was a good course, and government funded and all that, so I had no moral dilemmas, but it was so repetitive and it was hard to stay motivated, alone in my "office" with no one to talk to. I discovered that working from home doesn't shield you from all the other distractions of home so, although it's lovely to be able to put a load of washing on between phone calls, it's equally easy to be sidetracked into 'I'll just do that bit of weeding' or more likely 'I'll just have another cup of coffee' or even more likely 'Oooh, *Diagnosis Murder* is on' – oops, if you're working from home, disconnect the TV!

Then Alan started school, and was out for longer in the day. Good, I thought, I'll try and find a job that's a bit more rewarding and one where I can go OUT to work – it had been so long since I'd been OUT on my own, that going out to work was almost as exciting as going out on the town! So I found myself a secretarial job at the local university.

I suppose if I'd been concentrating more on the practical, I would have realised what it would be like – it was an old-fashioned, scruffy office in an institution that had clearly not seen much change in the last twenty years. Most of the office "girls", I soon learned, had been there for about twenty years, some since leaving school and some were related – mothers and daughters in the same office. Most hadn't worked anywhere else so had nothing to compare it with. It led to some interesting situations. I asked one day if I could take only half an hour for lunch and leave half an hour earlier, because I was having people over to dinner and I had some things to do. I thought it was a reasonable request. This was the conversation:

> Me: *Audrey, I wondered if I might be able to leave a little earlier this afternoon – say 4.30 instead of 5 – if I only take half an hour for lunch.*
>
> Audrey: *Well, I don't think that will be possible, but I'll ask Jennifer.*
>
> Me: *OK. What's the problem with it?*
>
> Audrey: *Well, I mean, if we let you do something like that, then everyone will want to do it.*
>
> Me: *I see – and what would be the problem with that?*
>
> Audrey: *Well, I don't know. I'll ask Jennifer.*

* * *

The answer was no. I protested, but was told that if I had needed to leave for something important they might have agreed, but as it was just because I wanted to have a nice time and enjoy myself (heaven forbid!), the answer remained no. I understood from the process that no one had ever had the temerity to ask for such a thing before and I vowed to be less honest next time – perhaps an elderly aunt's funeral would do the trick? Now, in other companies I'd worked for in the past, this kind of request was relatively common and the reply would often be 'Oh, just take the time off – as long as you finish everything that needs to be finished it will be fine'. It's no wonder, then, that in this sort of inflexible working environment, the question of my occasional absence due to child illness would be badly looked upon.

Anyway, once installed in this new job, with my apparently kind and charming boss, I felt for some time as if I'd fallen on my feet. The first few times Alan was ill, everyone was very sympathetic but it didn't last long. For although Alan isn't a sickly child, he managed to contract chicken pox twice, and of course, every time he was a little bit sick or got a slight case of the runs he became subject to his school's 48 hour rule – so I would have to keep him at home for two days at the very least, every time he was poorly. Patience started to run a little thin:

Conversation 2 (After being in the job for several months)

> *Work:*   *(Ring ring...) Hello?*
>
> *Me:*   *Hi! It's Julia*
>
> *Work:*   *Oh hi! You not coming in today?*
>
> *Me:*   *No, I'm afraid Alan's poorly again. He's got a tummy bug – I've got it too.*
>
> *Work:*   *OK. I'll let everyone know again. I'll put a form on your desk. Can you hand it in as soon as possible.*

> Me: *Sure. Thanks... bye.*
> Work: *Bye.*

*   *   *

Rather more curt and less sympathetic. I managed to persuade my mother to have Alan if he wasn't too sick, but I was always worried she might catch a nasty bug – it wasn't a happy solution. I almost gave up on booking holidays altogether, thinking I probably wouldn't have any leave left. Thank goodness for the Playscheme.

The Playscheme turned out to be a fairly good childcare choice. When I told the office "girls" (harbingers of doom, mentally trapped in the 1980s) that I was going to take Alan there, they all shook their heads and said how awful it was and how expensive. It wasn't, though. It was actually quite cheap by modern childcare standards and was very well organised. The only problem for me was that I always felt bad at having to carry on chasing Alan out of bed early in the morning and packing him off with his sandwiches and suncream, just like on a normal school day, when what he needed most of all was "down time". He made some friends, he was well catered for and he was safe, but he didn't always enjoy himself and yes, I felt the GUILT:

> Alan: *I don't want to go to playscheme. I hate it.*
> Me: *Oh, I'm sure that's not true. You had a lovely time yesterday making those bead things. And tomorrow you're going pond-dipping, on the bus.*
> Alan: *I HATE pond dipping. I want you to come.*
> Me: *I'd love to, sweetheart, but I can't. I have to go to work and earn money.*
> Alan: *You could just get some money from the bank machine. I want to stay at home with you.*
> Me: *Let's look at the programme for tomorrow. Oh look, tomorrow morning you're going to be making biscuits. That's your favourite.*

> *Alan: I hate making biscuits except with you...*

*   *   *

Oh dear! Sometimes there was no persuading him. I felt terrible making him go and leaving him there. If anything, he preferred the one-week Holiday Club at our local Congregational Church, where he knew the other children. We're not a church-going family, but Alan seemed to really take to the evangelistic view of God they were promoting at the club. It sparked his imagination, which must be a good thing, right? We used to have rather surreal conversations, normally somewhere public, where I would be frantically dealing with shopping and money, like at the supermarket check-out:

> *Alan: (looking around) Mum, do you know God is everywhere?*
>
> *Me: Is he really, darling? That's nice. (Under breath) Perhaps he could give me a hand then!*
>
> *Alan: God is love, Mummy.*
>
> *Me: Super – pass Mummy's handbag, please, Alan.*
>
> *Alan: Jesus was a fisherman, Mummy, like me and Grandad. Do you think Jesus ever caught a pike?*
>
> *Me: I expect so, dear.*

*   *   *

When I eventually felt Alan was settled enough in school, I decided that in order to cut out the holiday problems, I would "fall back". What is this "falling back" thing, you may ask? No, I wasn't going to have a nice lie down, although I really did feel like it! It refers to a stage in my life dating back years and years, when I first left school and didn't know what to do.

At school I only really liked one subject – from the moment I started at secondary school I became an official Francophile. I loved French. Starting from the age of 14, I went to France at every available opportunity. By the time I was 16, I was pretty fluent. When I left school, I went to Paris to be an au pair. It was while I was there, and in regular contact with my parents by letter (no email in those days!), that I decided I would be a French teacher. My parents' point of view was that it would be something to "fall back" on in later years, even if I decided not to teach immediately after college. I remember the shudder of horror I felt at the thought of having to "fall back" on something – a strategy that seemed to me then so completely devoid of positive thinking and totally lacking in spontaneity.

But I trained to be a French teacher anyway, having persuaded myself it was a good idea, and I got myself a job in a school where I taught French for four years. I didn't hate it, in fact I quite liked it, but it was an insular life and I remember how envious I was at the end of each year as pupils left to go on and do exciting and different things. I would be thinking 'I'd like to have a go at that' or 'I wish I could go there', and so eventually, I followed my instincts, chucked in my job and spontaneously (well, almost) went to work for the BBC. I completely forgot about "falling back" or any feelings I may have had either way about the prospect of doing it. The rest is history.

Several years on and faced with what on earth to do about earning an interesting living as a working single mum and what on earth to do with Alan during the holidays, when I would probably have to work, I necessarily began to examine my own resources, and the once repugnant possibility of "falling back" into teaching reared its not so ugly head. It was nearly 20 years since I'd given up teaching. The whole education system had been completely overhauled since then. I knew nothing about schools or teenagers any more.

I thought about applying to be a Teaching Assistant or Learning Support Assistant, but the hours didn't quite fit and the pay was very low and anyway, wasn't I a qualified teacher? I enquired about supply teaching, which I'd heard was very well paid. It was. But they wouldn't take me on the books unless I'd done a "Return to Teaching" course. I looked into it. It was something I could do part time. Frankly, I was so pleased I would be able to do something professional and reasonably well paid that, in the end, though I was going to be doing that awful "falling back" thing, I didn't give it a second thought. Totally lacking in spontaneity and devoid of positive thinking – yes, that's me! I didn't "fall back", I jumped! And while I was jumping I found another platform. I offered my services as a French teacher to primary schools in the area, and now I teach French two afternoons a week to small children, which is a joy. For one or two days a week, I suffer the slings and arrows of my local secondary school, where I do general supply teaching. Funnily enough, the kids there are always pleased to see me, but not usually for appropriate reasons! It's a thankless job, but I don't have to do it much and I often get at least a day, if not two days, at home every week, for which I'm grateful.

I (nearly) always take Alan to school. If I can't, then we have a child-minder who takes him for a small charge. My Mum or the child-minder picks him up from school and often, by the time they get home, I'm already there. It's a system that works all round. I earn enough to keep the wolf from the door, I don't get too tired, I do get some work satisfaction, I get to spend the holidays with Alan, Alan doesn't miss me, and I get to keep in touch with school and the parents of Alan's friends. It's taken a while to get the balance right. And of course, now, if Alan is ill and I have to ring and say that I won't be coming in, no one minds, because I simply don't get paid! I knew there had to be a downside!

*   *   *

By the way, I lasted a year and a half in the university job. My charming boss soon began to reveal his more boyish nature. There was one incident involving a missing library book. He called me in to his office having received a demand for a large library fine for a book not returned:

> My boss: *I'm really cross about this fine, Julia. What have you done with the book?*
>
> Me: *Well, let me see which book it refers to. Ah yes. I took all the others back, because I found them in your office, but I couldn't find this one, so I assumed you were still using it.*
>
> My boss: *Well you've definitely got it, because I certainly haven't. I've looked everywhere for it.*
>
> Me: *(knowing full well he hasn't looked anywhere) It's definitely not on my desk or on my shelves. I'll have another look in here if you like. Could you possibly have taken it home, or have you taken it with you on any of your trips?*
>
> My boss: *Of course not. I know what I did with it. I gave it to you.*
>
> Me: *OK. Well, I'll have another look and I'll go to the library and see if I can get the fine reduced.*

* * *

I did manage to get the fine reduced for a book that was apparently lost. He paid it with very bad grace, making it clear that I should really be the one paying it. Six months later, while my boss was on a short sabbatical in America, I had the following conversation with his daughter.

> Mary: *Hi Julia. Oh, by the way, while we were cleaning up at home the other day, my Mum and I found this library book that's really overdue. What would you like me to do with it?*

Me: *(note to self: this is definitely a moment when honesty is NOT the best policy)* Oh, well why don't you leave it on my desk and I'll take it back to the library.
Mary: OK.

*   *   *

I was very much put in mind of Alan having lost a toy and blaming it on me, while all the time it's right in front of his nose! Very soon after this incident, I enrolled on the "Return to Teaching course" and I came to the conclusion that having one small boy in my life, prone to having tantrums and making unreasonable demands, was quite enough for one woman and so I gave my boss the push. Serves him right! His next secretary only lasted three months...

7

Over my dead body...

I sat alone and anxious in a bright little room in the basement of the High Court, listening to the woman and her brand new husband trying to hide the truth about their circumstances. I could hardly breathe. The Judge's sound was muffled – wig slipped over the microphone? – I strained to understand her questions. All I could think of was, if the Judge had any even slightly barmy views about children being better off with two parents than with one regardless of their circumstances, I would be lost – or rather Alan would be lost!

Alan's birth mother – for it was she who was trying to reinvent herself for the benefit of the court – explained how she now regularly saw her first two children, from a former marriage that she had left for a man with a history of crimes against children – it didn't last and fortunately he wasn't Alan's father. She now had a new man in her life, her new husband, and suddenly she declared that she was pregnant again. I felt cold. She cried a little as she tried to explain why she wanted Alan. I felt unmoved as she pleaded to get "her" baby back. She talked about herself and her own feelings without once, I noticed, indicating that she had any idea of what things had been like for Alan, or how he might feel about being uprooted again. Her argument was that he would be better off with her because she was his birth mother, which of course she had always been, and it had certainly not proved to be better for him in the past! But would the court agree? She made quite a thing about having a new partner and providing Alan with a Daddy. 'Here we go,' I thought, 'playing the two parent-card!' I hoped the Judge had noticed her inability to consider what might be best for Alan. I felt I shouldn't be skulking in the cellar, listening to the proceedings from afar, as if I had something to be afraid of, when I should be up in court.

*   *   *

Now, a child's history and life story work are important, I know, but I can see how tempting it must be for an adoptive parent to simply forget about it and try to pretend a child is their natural child. They could count on the full collusion of their adopted children, who also wish they weren't adopted. Alan has always known he was adopted, although he has only recently been inclined to accept it. When he was small we often used to play this little game, which he invented, where he would hide up my jumper and pretend to be in my tummy. I would have to wait a while and then he would pop out and I would have to say something like: 'Oh – it's a beautiful little baby boy' and then I would have to cuddle him and coo over him and pretend to put a nappy on him. We probably played this game 10 times a day at one stage. From time to time he would ask me, out of the blue, it seems: 'Mummy, what does adopted mean?' But just recently, whilst waiting in an airport lounge, I was chatting to another mother when Alan suddenly exclaimed 'I'm adopted!'. I managed to remain calm, though I was staggered and cringed inwardly as the woman, clearly interested in what Alan had said, assumed it was a topic for general conversation and went on to ask some rather probing questions.

Not that it's a secret, but it's personal to Alan – his business. The fact is, Alan's birth mother tried to look after him for about six weeks before concerns about his welfare led to him being taken away and given temporarily to "Nanny" (an older woman who would eventually become Alan's long-term foster carer). He had bruises on his legs and it was suspected he may have been abused by someone his mother had left him with at the hostel where they lived. I think she left him a lot and when she was with him, she often ignored him. At three months he returned to his birth mother for a trial period. Before her time was up, Alan's birth mother gave him back to Nanny, realising that she couldn't cope.

At Nanny's house, Alan was the centre of attention – little golden haired, good-natured baby that he was. I imagine he didn't cry very much, because he would have learned during his first few weeks that his cries would probably be ignored. Nanny's household was busy and noisy, with many comings and goings. But it was full of love for Alan and he became a happy, if over-indulged, little boy. Nanny had two older adopted children, and another foster child just three years older than Alan, with horrendous behavioural problems. Although it was fairly chaotic, it was a relatively stable placement for Alan, until along came Mummy and whisked him away from everything he knew. How does a child survive all this upheaval? It's a miracle that they do and not surprising if they go on to develop a few little problems on the way.

After Alan had lived with me for a few months and we were pretty settled and getting to know one another, it was suggested that it would be a good thing for me to meet Alan's birth parents. Because I am an open-minded sort of person, and rather nosey, I agreed, although I was privately terrified. In fact, I ended up with three appointments – I was to meet Alan's mother, his father and his father's mother – Alan's paternal grandmother. I had read both parents' histories – they made for rather desperate and distressing reading. Alan's birth mother's life had always been a mess – she came from generations, it seems, of neglect, abuse, alcoholism and mental illness. She had a learning disability and had not really attended school regularly. As a child, she was in and out of care and ran away many times. Alan's birth father was from a rather different background – his father had been in the forces, they'd moved around a lot, he was very well educated, but in his early twenties he'd developed a mental illness, possibly provoked by drugs, and his life had changed beyond recognition. It was not exactly kismet that brought these two people together, but some form of fate caused their stars to collide briefly, resulting in Alan. Reading about them was the most depressing experience – surely, I thought, there must be more to them than just this black and white summary of their lives and problems. What are they like to talk to? Where does Alan get his sense of humour from? Who does he look like? Whose smile is that I see? Scary though it was, I went to meet them and I went on my own. I suppose I could have taken someone else along with me – a friend, my mum... but it didn't seem right to involve anyone outside our immediate family in something so private. Would it have been easier to face with a partner? Of course, but single adopters, not having that option, have to be prepared to face situations like this one on their own.

Alan's birth mother was clearly curious to see who had been looking after "her" little boy. She was nervous and jittery and cried a lot. She looked different from her photographs – thinner. She wanted to know about me and at the end of the interview she said how happy she was that Alan was living with me. She was a sad person, with a sad background. I felt great sympathy for her. I also understood what the social workers had told me about her, that she wanted Alan in theory, but that she couldn't handle the reality of looking after a child, day in day out. There was something about her that reminded me of Alan, though. He had her smile, her laugh, and the same expression in his eyes – yes, these were the positive things I would be able to tell Alan in the future when he wanted to know details.

The minute Alan's birth father walked into the room I could see that he was Alan's father – the way he walked, his face, his hair – all completely Alan. It was quite uncanny, the sort of resemblance, I guess, that people take for granted in "normal" families, but I was taken by surprise. He was quietly spoken (well, maybe not that much like Alan!), intelligent, articulate, had clearly accepted he would not be able to look after Alan and he made it quite clear that he was happy that Alan would be adopted by me. We talked about his early life and what he remembered about his childhood. I discovered he had been a talented sportsman before he was ill, particularly gifted at rugby – he was happy that he had recently been able to start playing hockey again. Alan was extremely well co-ordinated and very strong for a small child. I wondered if he would go on to be the sporty type like his father. Now, several years on, I believe he will. This year at his school sports day he came first in two races and third in his other one. He has also recently started playing rugby and has made an impression already.

Alan's birth grandmother was a very nice, ordinary woman, not too much older than me! She had been very ill, which is one of the reasons, she explained, that she and her husband had not been able to consider having Alan. I know that Alan's social worker had been quite critical of her decision, but I could understand how a couple in their fifties would balk at taking on a baby, from a union they knew nothing about, just as they were planning to retire.

They worried a great deal about their son, who was living in a supervised hostel, still unable to live on his own. She told me that she, too, had been adopted as a baby and that she had discovered it by chance aged 16. She said it had been a terrible shock and she went on to cut all ties with her adoptive family. She urged me to make sure that Alan was always told the truth, because the lies cannot be forgotten. I was happy to reassure her. She gave me a book of photographs of Alan's father. I was intrigued to see one photo of him as a baby, which could quite easily have been Alan. As I looked at pictures of Alan's birth father as a teenager and a young adult, it was like looking into the future. There is my son, in ten years' time, I thought.

Out of all this, I have had to sift what I can and can't tell Alan about his birth parents at each stage in his life. It's quite difficult. He asks such leading questions and all I can do is answer honestly and in a way I think he will be able to accept and understand. There is no point in making up stories or telling even slight untruths, because he will one day know the whole truth. I can't tell him gory details, because at the moment he would be too upset, and because he cannot be trusted to keep them to himself. In this small community, there is not always the kind of understanding one might hope for. He asked his birth mother's name – I told him. He asked his birth father's name – I told him that too and actually Alan's second name is his father's name. He was pleased to hear that.

But I'm often knocked slightly sideways by his questions, partly because they come when I'm least expecting them, like when I'm driving him to school:

> *Alan:* *Why can't I live with my birth mother?*
>
> *Me:* *She loved you very much, Alan, but she was poorly in a way that meant she wouldn't get better very quickly. So she gave you to Nanny (Alan's foster mother) to find you a new Mummy who'd love you and look after you.*

Alan: Is she better now?

Me: Well, she's a little bit better.

Alan: Can I go and see her?

Me: Perhaps when you grow up you'll be able to go and see her.

Alan: Why can't I go and see her now?

Me: (Starting to get a little worried) Because she's still poorly. Let's talk about it after school, shall we? Have you got your stuff?

*   *   *

Leading up to the adoption, I had agreed that Alan would have letter-box contact with both his birth parents and his paternal grandmother once a year. I'm sorry to say I'm not very efficient, so it doesn't always get done on time. I simply write a short letter about what Alan has been doing in the year – just news and little bits of information about him, and a photograph, so that his birth family are in touch with his life. In return they send letters to me. I read them and put them away and, when Alan is old enough to cope with them and read them himself, he will know more about them and, if he goes on to contact them later in life, there will be fewer shocks in store all round. I have not heard from Alan's birth father, but have had lovely positive letters from his grandmother, full of good wishes and news and I can see that they will be very helpful to Alan in the future. The letters from Alan's birth mother are something else – full of distress, imploring, full of 'I miss you terribly every day' and 'love always from your own mummy' – the kind of letters which are hard for me to read and will be extremely painful for him when he gets to read them because his birth mother has no clue about what's best for Alan and can only express herself in limited ways. I'm not saying she doesn't feel these things, but she writes them because she doesn't know what else to say. Oh, and she feels guilty, of course.

Alan has no conscious memory of his birth mother, but

ever since he was small and first understood that babies grow in their mummies' tummies, he has been very aware that he wasn't in mine. Occasionally he would say this to me:

Alan: I wish I had been inside your tummy, Mummy.

Me: I wish you'd been inside my tummy too. But I love you just as much as if you had been in my tummy!

*   *   *

And I know that Alan loves me, although something I was told in an adoption workshop when we were discussing the connection between birth mothers and babies, has always stayed with me. The social worker said, 'As an adoptive mother you have to accept that your child will never feel the same way about you as they do about their birth mother.' Hard words, but I can see that they are probably true. Nature organises things that way to protect babies, although things don't always work out. In a rage, Alan will sometimes say:

Alan: I hate you and I don't want to live with you any more.

Me: Oh dear! Well, I don't hate you. I love you.

Alan: I want to go and live with my birth mother because she's nicer than you.

*   *   *

I bite my tongue and think to myself 'Over my dead body' and if Alan is like many adopted children, that's probably what will happen. But hopefully, by then he'll be prepared.

*   *   *

Waiting alone beneath the Court room, just me and the machine that relayed the sound in a small windowless room – I've never felt more like a single mother than at that moment. There were plenty of people in the courtroom on mine and Alan's side – my solicitor, the social workers, the Guardian *ad litem* (now called the Children's Guardian)... I had to trust them but it was nerve-wracking, waiting for the Judge to make her decision. I wished I could have seen her face, which might have given me some clue as to what she was thinking. Meanwhile, Alan's birth mother cried, and she could think of no one but herself. Alan had been with me for a whole year – far longer than he'd ever been with her; I felt he was my son now. She'd had her turn and hadn't she done enough damage already?

When the verdict came I was incredibly relieved and happy and I'm not ashamed to say, because I think it's perfectly understandable, that while I would normally have felt compassion for Alan's birth mother and her painful story, on that particular day all I felt was gratitude and triumph. I wanted to celebrate.

Alan's social worker, Jackie, who's moved on to another post since, recently contacted us to say she'd bumped into Alan's birth mother in the street just a few weeks ago. She now has two more children with her new husband, apparently, and Jackie says she got the impression that the husband looked after the children. I'm glad he does.

8

And the Bafta goes to...

...Philip Seymour Hoffman? Who's he? Oh dear, does that make me sound like I don't get out too often? Well, there's a reason for that. I don't!

There was a time in my life, before Alan of course, when I would have known exactly who Philip Seymour Hoffman was. I would probably have followed his career and I would most certainly have seen his film and all the other films nominated for awards at both the Baftas and the Oscars. I would have recognised all the actors walking down the red carpet and I would have heard of all the designers whose dresses adorned the female stars.

Of course, back then, I would not have been able to sing you Barney's good night song, I would not have been able to name all four of the Tweenies, plus their dogs, nor would I have been able to do passable imitations of Sully (*Monsters Inc*) or Princess Fiona (*Shrek*). I guess it's a case of swings and roundabouts – quite literally, in this instance.

I feel I should warn you that this is the chapter that's most likely to sound like one long whinge. That's because I'm going to be looking back at how life was before Alan, with a certain amount of rose-tinted myopia, I expect, and thinking about things I would like to do now but can't, for various reasons connected to single parenthood. You may react like my friends and family do when I get into this mode. They tend to shake their heads and say, 'Well, it's what you wanted, isn't it?' Which is true. But you see, like all prospective parents, I didn't really know how life would be and I'm sure, as all parents inevitably do, I look back at my life before parenthood and remember fondly what it was like to be without responsibilities and ties. Isn't it only natural that occasionally I should think 'Oh wouldn't it be nice to just do whatever I feel like doing'?

* * *

The truth is I didn't really have a rip-roaring social life before Alan, simply because I worked long hours and when I wasn't working I was often rather tired. But, potentially, I could do whatever I wanted, whenever I wanted and I wouldn't have to worry very much about how much it cost. The greatest luxury, I think, of the single white female with a decent income is the potential for spontaneity. I could make snap decisions at the last moment to go out somewhere, for instance, to the cinema with friends after work, or out to eat; I could suddenly decide on a Friday to go away for the weekend; I could even suddenly decide to go away on a week's holiday if I wanted to; I could go out food shopping on a Saturday and come home with a new computer costing £1,000 without putting the mortgage payment in jeopardy (actually, I did do that once); I could stay up all Saturday night drinking, knowing that I would be able to stay in bed the next day if I needed to; I could buy a newspaper on Sunday morning (late) and know that I could spend the whole day reading it if I felt like it. Doesn't all that sound attractive? Yes it does, if a bit shallow.

Yet, despite the access to freedom my "singlehood" gave me, like many career-oriented people, my life revolved principally around work and I think everyone who leads that sort of life eventually reaches a point, precipitated by illness in my case, but it could be a particular birthday, it could be a death in the family, a crisis at work – whatever catalyst it takes – when they start to wonder if there isn't more to life. Ironically, when I found myself entrenched in motherhood, a similar situation arose – my entire life became Alan-centric and "I" started to disappear along with my personal aspirations. But, whilst I don't really miss my old life-style, there are aspects of my old life that I look back on with a certain amount of longing.

Shouldn't it be possible to carry on having a life when you have children, I hear you ask? We can all bring to mind friends who have children who apparently "dropped their sprogs" and simply carried on, barely missing a beat. I think it's fair to say, that although I didn't actually "drop" my sprog myself, I definitely don't fit into that category. For one thing, and I suspect this may be a very one-parent type of problem, Alan and I are a little team and so we "do things together". If I suddenly want to go off and do something on my own, I feel such a traitor leaving Alan behind, and he feels this treachery acutely – and lets me know about it. He's got used to me having no sort of life of my own, which is probably my fault, so if I need to go out to a meeting, or if I go out to the cinema or theatre with friends (it's not as if it happens very often!), he wants to come too and doesn't really understand why he can't. There isn't really a time when he's doing something else like, for example, going to stay with another parent for the weekend, as children of divorced parents do, when I could surreptitiously establish a separate social life. If he overnights with Grandma or Annie, though I try to build up the overnighting as the main event and Mummy going out somewhere as an afterthought, he still resents it mightily and it does feel somewhat like a betrayal. This is clearly awful and not a healthy situation, so I try not to let it put me off on the rare occasions when I get invited on my own. But then I do often find myself thinking 'Oh Alan would love this' when I am somewhere new without him.

One of the biggest problems for me in the past has been getting a babysitter. Occasionally, I ask my Mum to babysit, which means I don't have to pay, but I don't like to push my luck and take advantage of her, because she is my main emergency stand-by and because she's "getting on a bit" (she won't agree!). I don't like asking her to drive late at night, for instance. On other occasions, I ask Annie, who also doesn't charge. But Annie has teenage boys who have as many needs, if not more, than my seven-year-old, and they also have homework, which tends to surface just before bedtime and needs urgent, often lengthy, intervention. Also, her husband Matt is a music teacher and often works in the evenings, so Annie isn't able to leave her house. It's not that there's a shortage of potential babysitters. There are handfuls of teenage girls, suitable in age and disposition, in the village and who regularly babysit for other people I know, but there are two hurdles involved here. One, as you've probably guessed, is money. Paying for a night out AND a babysitter is mostly more than I can manage. The other problem is, if I don't get home until late (and that's generally the idea, isn't it?), how do I then get the babysitter home safely?

Recently the second problem has been solved, as my neighbour's daughter, now of babysitting age, has turned out to be a perfect babysitting gem. The first time she looked after Alan, I came home at 10pm, having been round to a friend's house for a drink, to find that Alan was fast asleep in bed, everything was in order, and the young lady in question was calmly getting on with her homework and watching TV. I should mention that she's the eldest of four children, two of whom are boys, so she's got the whole boy-thing taped. Alan, who loves teenage girls – he goes all baby-voiced and gooey and they in turn go all 'ahhh... isn't he cute' and want to pick him up – was perfectly happy for once to do as he was told. At the end of the evening, I simply stood at the front door and watched as the babysitter walked out of my gate and in through hers. Perfect!

The problem of money hasn't been solved. I have to factor it in to the cost of a night out and sometimes it's restricting. Mostly it means that when I do decide to splash out, I can't stay out too late, which is probably a good thing since these days if I don't get to bed at a decent time I suffer for a week and, consequently, so does everyone around me! If I had a partner, of course, I could join a babysitting circle and offer my services for free in return for services rendered. It would be a great thing, but is hardly the basis for a relationship, so things aren't likely to change any time soon!

Seriously, the "going out" issue is not a huge one for me. I miss the company of adults sometimes – the evenings can be a bit long and, although I've managed to avoid becoming addicted to the major soaps, I do watch too much "feel good" entertainment on TV rather than anything serious. But right now, while Alan is still young, everyday life takes up most of my energy, and there isn't too much left for organising myself into leaving the nest, even just for the evening. Actually, when Alan is tucked up in bed and finally asleep, I prefer just to chill out at home. This comfortable lethargy, though, doesn't stop me getting itchy feet whenever I watch travel shows and I think the thing I miss most is travelling and seeing new places, the "getting up and going", in theory at least, at the drop of a hat. It's fair to say I've been on holiday a lot in my life. I once put my job on hold for a year and travelled right round the world. It was fabulous. I've had a fantastic time camping and touring, whale watching, bear watching... In other words, I've had a ball. Some of the most memorable and happy times of my life have been on those trips. When

I chose to be a parent, I was realistic enough to know that I would have to accept that it was something I would probably never do again and I will admit that, if I allowed myself to sit down and think about it in any great detail, I would regret it.

But though I'm quite capable of having a good old moan, I'm not really one to mope, being a fairly pragmatic soul. Of course I know I could never afford to trail Alan around the world like that and of course I know it would be the most unsettling and frightening thing for him if I tried to. He needs the security of home, and besides, I've discovered I can give him a taste for adventure and travel without necessarily taking him anywhere exotic and, at least for now, I can satisfy whatever urges I have in the travel department too. For a start, I treat every trip as an adventure, whether we're going to the other side of the country for a camping trip, or whether we're just going into town to do some shopping. I make quite a big deal out of it, we always go equipped and I involve Alan in the preparations, so do we take a picnic, or wet-weather gear, do we need a bag to carry stuff, nets to catch fish, wellies and so on? This way he gets a feel for packing up and setting off and so do I. We also read adventure stories together – The Famous Five is a favourite of ours – we love how they're constantly going off on their bikes to have fun, pockets full of bits and pieces, such as a useful piece of string, a pencil stub, an old piece of chalk, a torch or a whole fruit cake, all essential gear if you get stuck down an old tin mine, with a complicated series of tunnels and only one way out! Well, it could happen!

When we do go on holiday somewhere marvellous – I say when, but we've only been once and that was Tunisia – I try to explore the cultural differences with him and let him experience things that I hope will help him to understand and embrace other cultures and not be afraid of diversity. So the trip to the local souk was as important for us, say, as the day we spent on the pirate ship (a really touristy day out on a real sailing ship with men dressed as pirates doing jolly dancing halfway up the rigging, brandishing cutlasses and trying to look fierce, and then serving a pirate lunch – barbecued meat and salad – all swashbuckling stuff and right up Alan's street). In the Tunisian market, Alan and I chatted to some of the people and bargained for our souvenirs together. It was fun. If you asked Alan what he most enjoyed, he would of course say 'the pirate ship', but I know the souk experience is in there somewhere, and that next time he's in a souk, when he's grown up and can pay for it himself, he'll know what to do (hopefully he'll be rich enough to buy his elderly mother a pretty carpet!) and he won't be afraid to venture slightly into the unknown.

The main solution I found to both the problem of not having much money and not being able to pay for a babysitter, was to entertain at home. It was with this in mind that I first established the Book Group, which met, until recently, every month at my house. We chatted – sometimes about the book some of us had read – and had a few glasses of wine. It was very pleasant. We also occasionally have people round to the house, just for coffee, or for dinner, or even to stay for the whole weekend.

Now, I've always loved entertaining, but these days I'm very much preoccupied with the "state of the house" and, annoyingly, if I haven't given it as much attention as I feel I should, I often find myself apologising; I wish I didn't do that. I wish I could just say 'they'll have to take us as they find us' – but the thing is, there are times when it's quite difficult to find us, so untidy does the house become! That's an exaggeration, of course, or at least I hope it is. But whereas in the past I'd be fairly confident about the tidiness of my abode, these days I can't always tell what might have suddenly appeared and be lurking ready to shock and surprise the hapless visitor, or what might have been missed by my fairly eagle-like eyes. I normally give the bathroom regular inspections on days when we're expecting guests, so I'm able to deal immediately with anything that looks nasty but I know is harmless, like lumps of brown paint, or chewing gum covered in cat hairs.

Sometimes I can deal with severe untidiness by simply shutting doors – my office is a prime example. It's nearly always untidy because if I'm running around tidying the rest of the house, I have a tendency to open the office door, throw something in, shut the door quickly again and pretend it doesn't exist! It's like a kind of black hole in the house: perfect, except for when I need to get to my desk, when I have to tread gingerly amongst the piles of (potentially) important paperwork and other debris in order to avoid a major avalanche. Sometimes a gentle wading motion helps me to reach the chair, so that I can sit down and actually use my computer (so much for working from home!). I should point out to anyone reading this who hasn't had a reply to a letter or a final demand that I know exactly where their correspondence is...it's in a pile of paperwork I picked up from the kitchen table when the Book Group were due to come over one evening. It's on the floor between the cat's basket and a box of photographs I brought up from the dining room and next to a box of marbles and unidentifiable plastic bits that Alan left on the stairs! You see! I'm totally on top of things.

Why is any of this more pertinent to being a single parent than a couple? Well, I would say because when we're entertaining, I have to do all the preparation myself. I think some of my married friends would say, so what's new? But at least if you're a couple one of you can serve drinks while the other burns the hors d'oeuvres – whereas I have to burn the hors d'oeuvres all by myself, while the visitors have to serve the drinks, and then there's no hiding the glass that Alan decided to keep worms in, is there?

*   *   *

I think the main difference between before Alan and after Alan is that before Alan I was single, on my own and had a single person's lifestyle. Now I'm single, and I have a married person's lifestyle, without the advantages and disadvantages of a marriage. But mostly, I'm not on my own any more and the fact is that Alan is by far and away the person I most want to be with, so the sacrifice of giving up going out is not ultimately a great one. It's fun to go out sometimes with friends and mostly I enjoy it, but I want to do different things now and if I was to return to the way I was before, money or no money, I don't think I would be happy. When you're a parent, everything changes, even the way you want to spend your time, and the reason for that is down to a mixture of changed horizons and different physical stresses.

I always remember, years ago, being very impatient with a friend of mine who had young children, when we went out to the cinema one evening. She didn't get out much, so I imagined I was doing her an enormous favour, but she wasn't particularly enthusiastic about the film and didn't seem to want to discuss it much afterwards either. I felt quite put out and I must have tackled her about it because I remember her saying, 'I'm sorry. Somehow I can't stop myself from falling asleep. I'm sure it was a great film.' These days, of course, I understand completely. It's the sleep deprivation thing. Sit a mother down in a warm, darkened room, in a lovely comfy seat and play noise that doesn't absolutely require her immediate and urgent attention and Bingo! She's away. I've had some of my best snoozes in cinemas, particularly during the many dreary cartoons with thin plots and terrible dialogue that I've had to endure with Alan lately. I find the punchy music and snappy script delivery (celebrity voices) filters down to a rather soothing barking noise as you gradually drift off! Philip... Seymour... Hoffman... Philip... Seymour... woofman... Philip... woof... woof... woof.

9

'Can I have a word with you?'

Nothing is more guaranteed to make a small family feel miles smaller than making it face adversity on its own – in my case, running the gauntlet of the school playground each day, waiting for the children to come out accompanied by a stony-faced or (equally chilling) "understanding" teacher, or facing up to parents whose darling son or daughter has been clocked by my son! People have said to me 'Oh, it's just boys, don't worry' or 'He'll grow out of it soon enough,' but there are approximately 150 other boys in my son's school, so how come it's just me that has to talk to the teacher at the end of the day and, as time passes, I have to ask 'just WHEN is Alan going to grow out of this?'

Here's an extract from a report made by a Behaviour Therapist at the Nursery School Alan attended before coming to live with me:

> ' ...the children's centre has been open to children for 36 days (Monday to Friday) and Alan has attended for 21 days. There have been 11 actual bites to other

*children and five attempted bites. There is one record of
an attempted pinch to other children. Therefore there
have been a total of 16 bites or attempted bites in 21
days…The incidents have tended to occur when he is
playing alongside other children on the carpet or whilst
playing with outdoor play equipment… 8 of the 16
incidents have occurred struggling to get a desired toy.
On one occasion Alan bit another child who was crying
close to him. On the remainder of occasions staff have
felt the behaviour has occurred for no apparent reason
or the person recording it did not directly witness the
event.'*

*   *   *

She went on to say that she was fairly convinced that Alan
was not getting enough sleep and was very tired and
crotchety. I knew that life in his foster family was fairly
hectic, and that he didn't have a regular bedtime, or for
that matter any routines at all. In my innocence, I believed
that once he was used to proper routines, this sort of
behaviour would stop. I was wrong. It's improved in that I
can normally trust him to play with another child for a
couple of hours without incident, but he regularly hits and
punches at school, he hits me at home occasionally and
this summer, while we were camping, he bit a child he
hardly knew, on the face. These are pretty much the only
times I seriously wish that I was not alone. I have to deal
with upset parents on my own and try to placate them; I
have to console the injured child; I have to chastise or
punish Alan in a fairly public sense; I have to try to
understand, talk to Alan and comfort him (because he's
often very upset as well); and then I have to steel myself to
face the parents again the next day. There's no one to say
'it'll be OK' or 'it's not your fault – you're doing a great
job' or even 'don't worry, I'll take him to school today';
and no one to say 'we'll get through this, you and I'. It's

just me and Alan and an ongoing problem.

*   *   *

Behaviour is a difficult thing to handle when there's only one of you. It requires you to split yourself in two – you have to discipline and nurture at one and the same time. This is particularly hard if you are the target of a nasty tantrum. When Alan first came to live with me he was extremely compliant. 'This is a piece of cake,' I thought. I convinced myself I must be a very capable parent indeed and that the whole thing was going to go just swimmingly. I read the report from his nursery school and, frankly, disregarded it.

About three months after Alan came to live with me we went to Annie and Matt's house for dinner. Alan played with their boys and had a great time. It was a lovely and successful evening. But when it was time to go home, my lovely compliant little boy suddenly turned into this snarling, spitting, biting little demon. I was shocked and very upset. Annie and her family were shocked too. I reminded her about it recently:

> Me: *Do you remember that evening when Alan first had a temper tantrum? What did you think about that?*
>
> Annie: *I thought I was glad he was going home with you! No, really, it was quite scary, wasn't it? He was so angry and red in the face. I was worried he was going to hurt you.*
>
> Me: *He DID hurt me. He gave me a terrific bite on the shoulder. He managed to break the skin through my clothes. Had you every seen anything like that before?*
>
> Annie: *Nothing that violent, I don't think. My boys were never like that. I did start to wonder how you were going to manage.*

*   *   *

Fortunately he was very small then. Between us we managed to get him out of the house and into my car, but he was still wrestling with me and I was in total shock. I remember that, having calmed him down, I sat dazed and wondering how on earth I was going to deal with this if it went on forever.

It hasn't gone on forever, but he does still have violent outbursts, which often take me completely by surprise. As recently as last year, he had such a tantrum; I had to shut myself in my office in order to avoid him punching and kicking me. He proceeded to throw everything from his bedroom out onto the landing. Finally, because I really couldn't cope any more, I called Annie. She came and took him away, while I calmed down and tried to get a grip on myself.

> Me: *I felt like a real failure when I had to call you to come and take Alan away. It felt like the worst thing to do, in a way, because it was sort of fuelling his sense of insecurity, and it was also rewarding his bad behaviour, because then he could come over and play with your boys on their playstation.*
>
> Annie: *I don't think he looked on it as a reward. He was very sheepish. I think he knew he'd gone too far. Matt and I certainly made sure he knew that we disapproved of what he'd been doing.*

* * *

After a couple of hours, I went and fetched him home. He was calm and so was I. We had a hug and a chat about what had happened and then together we tidied away all the things he'd thrown out of his bedroom onto the landing. He's never gone so far over the top again.

Not having another adult in your corner is tough – no one to say 'don't talk to your mother like that,' or 'you go downstairs and have a cup of tea, I'll deal with this'. How liberating it must be to be able to simply walk out of the door, knowing that another adult was taking care of things for the time being! But I have to be strong, firm Mummy – sometimes angry, "shouty" Mummy – and then I have to be kind, forgiving Mummy, cuddly and 'it's alright now' Mummy. It's enough to do your head in. I have every sympathy for single mums who "let their kids get away with anything". Dealing with behaviour problems is just exhausting. It would be so easy to give in! I had this conversation with Carol, my single adopter contact provided through my adoption agency:

> Me: *There are some days where I seem to turn into a constant nag. I'm on poor Alan's case all day. It's as if I'm so worried his behaviour will be awful that I overcompensate and correct everything he does.*
>
> Carol: *I think the answer is not to aim your sights too high. You need to tackle issues one at a time, and yes, I think you have to let some things go by. No child is completely perfect.*
>
> Me: *You're right. I'm going to have to try to deal with the really bad things and ignore some other stuff.*
>
> Carol: *And remember, some of his behaviour is deliberately geared to getting your attention, so turning a blind eye is probably the best policy in those cases.*

* * *

So I do sometimes turn a blind eye to behaviour that is just on the limits of unacceptable, but unfortunately other people don't always appreciate this. Being constantly concerned about Alan's eating – or non-eating – I tend to concentrate on encouraging him to eat rather than on how he's eating, which sometimes results in some fairly choice table manners. He doesn't throw food, or spit it out, or try to eat soup with his fingers (not often, anyway) and I usually ignore all but the worst infringements, simply because I don't want to put him off eating. But recently, while staying with some friends, poor Alan found himself under attack for not eating "properly" and these friends made it clear they felt table manners mattered and that Alan should do better. I smiled nicely and told an astonished Alan to sit up and hold his fork properly and later, when the washing up was finished, I apologised to my friends and tried to explain to them that with Alan I tried not to set the bar too high. I think they understood – well they invited us back, so it can't have been too bad!

The key to keeping hold of your sanity is not to panic. When I begin to think 'oh God it's all awful and it's never going to get any better,' I have to force myself to take a step back and then to have a conversation with someone sensible. I'm lucky that Annie is such a person:

> Annie: *When you look at how Alan is now compared with how he was a few months after he came to live with you, he's a completely different boy, isn't he?*
>
> Me: *I suppose so. It's hard to remember.*
>
> Annie: *And at school now they notice and report every little incident to you – they're looking for trouble. But the incidents don't seem to be so serious, do they?*
>
> Me: *Yes it's true – there are lots of little things, but he doesn't react quite so badly now…*

* * *

Perspective is a good thing. But it's not always easy. I remember when Alan was still at pre-school, one Sunday evening, quite late, he was in bed and there was a knock at the door. It was the mother of one of Alan's classmates. To this day I am sure that if she'd thought I had a husband sitting on the sofa beside me she would not have arrived all guns blazing, threatening me with her irate in-laws and demanding that I "do something". But she was very cross and I was fair game. Alan had badly scratched her little boy's face at a party the previous day. Although I'd been at the party, I had not been aware – nor had anyone else to my knowledge – that Alan had done this thing. I was mortified obviously and, knowing the little boy in question, I was certain it was the truth. Photographs had been taken, school contacted, as many parents as possible had been informed – it was horrible and alarming and I felt terribly alone.

The next day when I asked Alan about the incident, he eventually confessed, but didn't seem to know how it had happened or why. I made it clear to him that he should never hurt another child and I made a public gesture, by banning Alan from a party the following weekend. I didn't know what else to do. As time went on, this became just one, although it was the worst, of numerous incidents and it may seem odd that something wasn't done immediately. Well, Alan was not all about hurting people and being obnoxious. The rest of the time he was lovely – he had plenty of friends, he was quite popular (not with the parents, of course), and his teachers seemed to like him, in spite of his problems. The other children knew him well and seemed to accept that sometimes Alan behaved badly. He was not ostracised and was perfectly happy to go to school each day – in fact he would run – he still does – the last part of the way.

Nonetheless, complaints were almost daily. It began to get ridiculous; I was even expected to account for why Alan wouldn't sit still on his chair in class! But the hitting incidents worried me tremendously. They often happened at playtimes, when the children were supposedly supervised, but no one was able to tell me exactly when, or what the circumstances were. After two years of cringing in the playground after school, I decided to take action.

Action, like discipline, takes willpower. I could tell you that I strode into school, grim faced and determined and made things happen. But it wasn't quite like that. It was more like kicking a ball through very sticky mud – it was hard work and once the ball reached the next player, the momentum was a bit lost! We talked about strategies: the school promised to instigate a "strategy" for Alan, which would involve star charts and a weekly chat with the head. The head promised to reward Alan's good behaviour by giving him privileges, like having one of his drawings displayed in the head's office. In return, I promised to support their "strategy" at home. This sounded great. I felt some progress was made. It worked, to my knowledge, for about a week! I felt thwarted and as if I had not been taken seriously by Alan's school. It was disappointing.

But, now that I'd got my teeth into it, I decided to continue. Early advice from Alan's social worker, when I'd discussed his biting problems and suggested getting help from the mental health services, had prevented me from contacting them. 'You don't want to start going down that route...' she had warned. How ridiculous that advice now seemed. Alan was already well on his way to serious trouble and he needed help. So I contacted our family doctor, the Child and Adolescent Mental Health Service (CAMHS) and my own adoption agency, whose advice and support were brilliant. Things started to happen. First, the school nurse went to Alan's school and watched him at playtimes. But it wasn't very professionally done. She didn't really see anything and she wondered what all the fuss was about. Then an adoption specialist from the CAMHS arranged a meeting with me and Alan's teacher. She gave the teacher – whom she later described as reluctant – some ideas on how to respond to Alan when he displayed anti-social behaviour (strategies again – they lasted a couple of weeks, but that's all). Finally, I took Alan to a paediatrician, who talked to him and then went in to school to observe him. Frankly, after all we'd been through, I didn't really need a professional to tell me that 'Alan is socially awkward, doesn't always understand social situations and doesn't always respond appropriately'. This I knew. However, it was helpful to the school, I think, to understand that it wasn't enough to tell Alan NOT to do something; they also had to tell him or show him WHAT to do instead. They needed to know, as did I, that positive rewards would be helpful, but that taking things away from him, such as stars from his star chart, would be unhelpful. We all needed to be told that Alan did not have anything diagnosable wrong with him. I needed to be told that his social awkwardness would improve with time – he would learn. Thank goodness! It really took the pressure off. I can now see that he is improving and that the difficulties are starting to disappear.

Alan has always been unwilling to discuss his behaviour with me. He finds it very distressing to have to face up to his social mistakes. Intellectually he knows how to behave, but somehow, during the first two years of his life he failed to internalise any kind of behaviour code – or at least any kind of acceptable behaviour code. I have learned that as a tiny child he would have been preoccupied with surviving – making sure he was looked after and that he would be OK – and so would not be picking up signals and clues about social behaviour, like other children normally do. I think it's getting better and that he is starting to put the brakes on his behaviour by himself. But progress is slow. If I'd had a partner would we have managed to get to grips with this earlier on? Discussing the issues together may have brought things to a head sooner. My friends and family are wonderful and helpful, but they're not implicated in the same way. They also don't see so much of the behaviour in question. Would Alan's behaviour have been more easily modified with two parents as role models? Possibly.

* * *

In fact, my best ally in the battle to remain calm about "what goes on at school" has turned out to be my Mum. I have occasionally taken her with me to parents' evenings, for example, where whilst I would have a tendency to hear nothing but 'it's all awful and a disaster' and probably, 'it's all your fault,' my Mum would hear a rather more accurate version of the report – it's all down to perspective again, you see.

A few weeks ago, when my Mum was picking Alan up from school, an irate mother of one of Alan's classmates bore down on her in a rather aggressive way and said 'Can I have a word with you?' Before my Mum had a chance to respond, this mother launched into a story of how Alan had been stealing her daughter's hat and not letting her have it back. Afterwards my Mum told me she couldn't believe this woman was getting involved in such a silly childish incident – the sort of thing that happens all the time when children play. Anyway, my Mum waited for the woman to stop her tirade, and in her calmest most matter-of-fact voice said, 'And does your daughter have her hat back now?' To which the mother replied 'Yes'. 'Well that's all right then, isn't it?' said my Mum, pleasantly. The mother, taken aback and somewhat deflated, agreed. (Next day she apologised to me for attacking my mother!) That was fantastic, I thought. Now why can't I do that?

10

How not to "make it an issue" and stay well

By the time Alan arrived, I had already decided that, as food was an important part of his growth and development, we were going to be organic and I was going to cook. I spent ages searching shops for recipe books and eventually found a lovely one with super pictures and pages of what seemed like wonderful advice. After reading the introduction, I really wanted to believe that my toddler would think that "a tasty fruit bread, combining grated apples or carrots with dried fruit and citrus zest" would make a fabulous breakfast!

I bought the book and decided the first meal I would make from it would be macaroni cheese – one of Alan's favourites, so his foster mother had told me. I followed the recipe meticulously. Three saucepans (I kid you not – this is what the recipe required) and an oven-proof dish later, I served my masterpiece, all bubbling and golden, to my golden-haired boy. He took one look and burst into tears:

    Alan: *(sobbing) but... I... don't... like... it!*

    Me: *It's macaroni cheese darling, look, it's lovely.*

> *You do like it.*
Alan: *(prodding with fork) It's got bits in it. I don't like them.*
Me: *It's just lovely, nice bits that taste yummy. Try some...?*
Alan: *It ... smells... all... funny...*

* * *

Now, as you may have guessed, I am a woman who appreciates her food. In the face of a child not wanting to eat, I found myself rather nonplussed. Early on, during a routine visit to the health visitor, we discussed the issue of Alan's appetite:

Me: *I'm a bit concerned about Alan's eating. He never seems to be hungry. Should I be worried?*
Health Visitor: *From what you've told me, he doesn't seem to eat much at any one sitting, but he seems to be eating the right things. I should try and concentrate on little and often.*
Me: *I see.*
Health Visitor: *He looks very well, and he seems to be growing well. The most important thing is not to "make it an issue".*
Me: *Ah! Right.*

* * *

Sounds easy, doesn't it? But what exactly does it mean? Does it mean encourage him to eat a little of everything, while not demanding he cleans his plate? Does it mean just let him get on with it, and eat or not eat, depending on how he feels? Does it mean only cooking food that he likes and then finding he doesn't apparently like it any more, throwing it away and not minding...? Quite quickly, not "making it an issue" became a huge issue for me and, being such a small family, with only me as a role model, it was probably an even bigger issue. If there had been two adults, and possibly older children, I have a feeling that Alan would have tended to go with the flow more readily. Instead, he seemed to take the view that just because I did something, I wasn't necessarily representative of the world as a whole. I guess he had earlier role models, with a rather different outlook to mine and he simply was not used to anyone taking any notice of what he ate and when. Apparently, as a tot, he would help himself from the fridge if he was hungry and I had seen for myself that the foster family didn't have a dining table – apparently 70 per cent of households don't – so mealtimes, when they happened, were a question of perching on a barstool in the kitchen and eating quickly and largely without supervision, I suspect.

From the start I felt it would be important for us to establish proper mealtimes. This is how it was in my own family; it was always part of our family routine that everything stopped for tea, so to speak. It meant there were regular times when we all came together and took stock of each other. We could discuss our day, talk about what we'd be doing, make sure we were all OK. It worked. I'm sure we weren't always particularly gracious, my brother and I, but we understood that the food in front of us was what was on offer and we ate it.

With Alan, keeping this going has been a bit of a battle. My son's table manners still leave much to be desired, but most of the time we manage to sit at the table, which has been properly laid, and we eat a meal together...or rather I eat, and Alan sometimes eats. Although there are just the two of us, I'm convinced this routine has helped us to become a family and it has helped Alan to learn to eat something other than sweets and cake. I'm not sure if it has helped not to make food an issue because, of course, sitting opposite him at every mealtime, the temptation is to be fairly focused on Alan and what he is or isn't doing with his food. From time to time, this means I've just been unable to stop myself from getting cross, showing my frustration and, quite frankly, making a huge great ISSUE of the whole thing.

Me: *Eat your food, Alan.*

Alan: *(Says nothing – stares away into the distance)*

Me: *Alan, eat some food.*

Alan: *I don't like it.*

Me: *(getting impatient) Alan, it's sausages and beans. What do you mean you don't like it?*

Alan: *It tastes funny.*

Me: *(starting to get cross) Don't be ridiculous. It tastes of sausage and beans. Now EAT.*

Alan: *(picks a bit and eats a really tiny piece)*

Me: *(Cross) Alan!*

Alan: *(shouting) I HAVE EATEN SOME AND I DON'T WANT ANY MORE.*

*   *   *

Oh dear! Not a very successful way of dealing with things, as you can see. But when you've put a lot of thought into a meal, spent a long time preparing it and you KNOW your child likes what it contains, it's hard not to react when they turn up their little noses and ask for biscuits! Perhaps if you have three children, two of whom eat the food and only one resists you don't feel quite so emotional about it – because it is emotional, isn't it? Perhaps it's just Alan's bad luck that he's my only customer. In the end, I've resorted to various strategies, which little by little, have worked to a degree. I've tried only giving him food I know he's guaranteed to eat – such as sausages, chicken and carrots. But he even manages to be capricious about these dietary staples. Some sausages are too "minty", according to Alan – by this he means spicy. Eventually, I decided that if he wouldn't even eat things I knew he liked, I might as well give him things he might not like, but which I DID like (after all, I eat in this restaurant too!) and not worry whether he ate them or not. I would make sure he had healthy snacks and that he had enough to eat, but it seemed pointless to pander to his whims, which were, after all, so whimsical!

So I started introducing other foods gradually and began trying not to care, or at least looking as if I didn't care, if he simply pushed them to one side. I also applied a little bit of psychology. Because chicken was usually OK with Alan (although it did rather depend on what it looked like), I started calling all meat chicken, so we had chicken pork, chicken beef, chicken lamb – all of which he would quite happily eat, believing it all to be chicken. He loved rice, so I introduced couscous by calling it couscous rice. Now he loves couscous, I've dropped the pretence! What was astonishing is that once he realised I wasn't going to make a fuss, he began eating all sorts of things, and apparently liking all sorts of things that I would never have imagined he would like. For instance, he loves chicken korma and chilli con carne (particularly if made with baked beans instead of kidney beans) and he's very partial to broccoli and courgettes. One day, without making any comment, I gave him raw carrot sticks with his lunch, and he simply demolished them. Also, having declared his hatred of tomatoes, he was quite happy one day to eat cherry tomatoes, which he now takes in his lunch box to school every day. I'm positive that if I asked him if he liked raw carrot and tomatoes he would say a definite no. So, basically, I don't ask.

Of course, all this concern about our food is really concern about our health. We're fortunate that despite his attitude to food, Alan is generally very healthy. He doesn't have asthma or eczema and he doesn't have any other long-term health problems. He doesn't pick up much in the way of bugs – although tummy bugs are apparently rife at school, Alan has only been sick a handful of times and never enough to warrant more than a couple of days at home. He's had chicken pox twice, the odd cold but nothing more serious.

I, on the other hand, though I eat healthily and well, have never been more ill! Since Alan came to live with me, I have found myself regularly succumbing to bugs – and I don't just mean the microscopic ones! I've had colds, coughs, tummy upsets, chest infections and conjunctivitis, but also head lice, cat fleabites and even scabies. For the first time in my life, since I was a child anyway, my doctor knows me by sight and calls me by my first name without having to look at his notes! If Alan goes down with anything, thankfully it's over within a few hours or a couple of days at the most. But when it's passed on to me, for some reason I'm struck down for days on end and even weeks! It was this summer that I picked up scabies – did Alan have it or not? It was never established and he certainly had no symptoms. I, on the other hand, became covered in a nasty, itchy, allergic rash. Although the scabies was quickly dealt with – one application of smelly ointment does the trick - the rash wouldn't go away and lasted right through the summer from July to October. Very nice, thank you! One thing I can say for sure is it's hard not to "make an issue" of someone pouring scorn on your cooking when you've spent a whole sleepless night trying not to scratch!

Joking aside, illness for a single parent is a serious practical problem, as well as a difficult emotional thing to deal with on your own. Twice I've started new jobs and Alan has contrived to be poorly on my first day. Even I don't have the gall to phone a new employer and take the first day off sick! Fortunately, my Mum has been able to stand in on those days and because Alan has never been very poorly, I have been able to leave him without too much difficulty, while being very aware that his "illness" on these occasions is probably due to a certain amount of insecurity. Presently, my working life allows me to have some flexibility, so that if Alan is ill I can easily stay at home. However, I don't get paid if I don't work, so it's still not a perfect scenario.

If Alan is ill at home during the daytime, I have a very useful medical resource – Annie is a nurse and is often called upon to help me determine what's wrong. Does she mind? I asked her:

> Me: *Do you mind me ringing up and asking you about Alan when he's poorly? It's just that I have no idea sometimes what's wrong, or if there's anything wrong, and what with you already having two boys and being a nurse...*
>
> Annie: *No I don't mind at all. It's worrying when there's something wrong and you don't know what to do. I can see that. And I've seen most of these things before.*
>
> Me: *And thank god you're always so calm about it.*
>
> Annie: *(laughing) I might not be so calm if you called me at 3 in the morning!*

* * *

Actually, it was Annie's husband, Matt, who answered the phone one evening when Alan had been sick. He'd started throwing up in his bedroom and as I carried him along the landing to the bathroom, he managed to spread vomit right along the wall – about twenty-five feet of vomit in all! He was hysterical and, frankly, so was I. This is a good example of the basic problem with being a single parent. You can't hold the child and clean up the sick. Annie was out, so Matt came round, and while I held a frightened and sobbing Alan, Matt cleaned up the vomit. That's true friendship and it's exactly what you need from your support network. Would they actually have come out and helped me if I'd called at 3am with a similar problem? Probably, although I'm glad to say that I haven't had to test it out.

Fortunately for us all, someone invented NHS Direct and there's nothing more calming than being patronised by a motherly nurse who's heard it all before when you're panicking on your own in the middle of the night. Sometimes, if I'm having trouble sleeping, I'm tempted to ring them up just for a chat. But if Alan has a temperature, or in situations like the night he found my handbag, rifled through it and found the antihistamine tablets I'd carefully concealed in a secret pocket, NHS Direct is second to none. He hadn't taken any tablets, by the way, but it was helpful to know what to do if he had. No one wants to be thought an over-anxious mother, so at 2.30am, when your child's temperature seems to be off the scale and you don't know what to do, it's good to be able to talk to someone sensible and not to dial 999 and waste tax payers' money.

Wonderful as they are, though, even NHS Direct won't come round and sit up all night with a sick child. And lack of sleep for all single parents, not just single adopters, is a killer. Alan now sleeps very well, but for several years he was wakeful, and it was quite usual for me to be up at least once or twice in the night. It's no wonder I got so run down that every little bug from Alan's school made a beeline for me. In fact, I can see quite a substantial gap in the market here – perhaps one day, in a few years' time, when I've finally caught up on my sleep, I may go into business running a Wakeful Child service. At one stage, Alan would regularly wake up at 3am. How nice it would have been to employ one of those nice NHS Direct matrons to call in at that time each morning and just help Alan get back to sleep, so that I could snooze unaware and wake the next morning all fresh and rested, instead of frazzled and grouchy! I've met quite a few grouchy and frazzled looking mothers during the school run in the morning.

When I'm ill, and I have had a few infections which have meant I really needed to stay in bed, the practicalities can be extremely tough. One morning, though, when I woke up with gastric flu and found myself having to get Alan ready for school whilst throwing up in a bucket, another unexpected problem reared its head. Alan understands that his birth parents, both of whom have mental illnesses, could not look after him, because they were too poorly. About a week after the morning when I'd been ill, Alan's teacher asked to speak to me. Alan's behaviour had been particularly bad and she was wondering whether anything had happened to set him off. I couldn't think of anything. Later that day a social worker from my adoption agency phoned to ask if I would take part in a course they were running. We were just chatting about Alan and about life story work:

Social worker: *So, what have you explained to Alan about his birth parents and why they gave him up?*

Me: *Well, usually I say they loved him very much, but they were poorly and couldn't look after him.*

Social worker: *You know what, I can see why you say that, but I think you need to tell him a bit more. Otherwise, if you're poorly, he may start to worry that you're going to give him away...*

It was one of those light-bulb moments! How stupid of me! I realised that having seen me poorly, Alan was indeed worried about losing me. We talked about it. He was very anxious, but seemed relieved when I reassured him that I was never, ever going to give him up. His behaviour improved and I learned a lesson!

*   *   *

Two heads, it's generally agreed, are better than one and maybe, because I'm on my own, it sometimes takes me longer to cotton on to things. Perhaps more mistakes are made. Perhaps it's harder to see the bigger picture. The macaroni cheese incident was a definite lesson learned the hard way. After about half an hour, with Alan crying and me trying to cajole, I decided, in the interests of my sanity and not "making it an issue" to give up. I boiled some pasta and covered it in grated cheese. Alan's little face lit up, not in victory, but with pleasure. He downed the lot without a murmur. And the organic children's cookery book? After I'd finished the washing up, I threw it away!

11

How to pitch a tent on your own and keep smiling

Picture the scene – it's pouring buckets of rain, it's unseasonably cold. I've just driven for three hours in rain so intense that several times I've been forced to pull over. I'm tired, because last night we slept – that's a joke because I didn't sleep – in hard bunk beds, all twisted up in sheet sleeping bags, in a youth hostel. The purpose of this exercise was so that I wouldn't have to drive for seven hours and then pitch the tent. Right now, as I'm soaking wet and bailing water out of bits of the tent still lying on the ground, I'm wishing we hadn't bothered! In the car, keeping dry, is Alan, who has refused point-blank to help me. It's just as well he's not around to hear what's coming out of my mouth, because it isn't very ladylike! Across the campsite there's a man sitting in his car watching me. I'm tempted to "wave" at him in a rather explicit way. Instead I soldier on, whacking tent pegs vindictively and stretching guy ropes to within an inch of their lives until, utterly exhausted and streaming with water, the tent, Gawd bless 'er, is finally up. I lay down the ground sheet, blow up the mattress (I'm SO glad I splashed out on an electric pump this year – my leg muscles haven't got a pump left in them!), make the bed, warm up some milk on our camping stove for hot chocolate, we put on our pyjamas and get into bed, even though it's three in the afternoon, just to try to get warm. One question is uppermost in my mind: is this a holiday?

* * *

Small families can do just as many things together as large families. But they can't always do the same things. Alan and I on our own would find it hard to manage by ourselves in a five-a-side football match, say. There are two other great disadvantages. One is that things are as expensive, if not more expensive, for two than for three – and holidays are a prime example. As a family of two, you can often find yourself paying for two adults, plus paying for under-occupancy of a hotel room. This is one of the reasons we go camping. The other disadvantage is that many activities we can afford to do, inevitably involve me in a lot of work – carrying heavy stuff to and from the car, heaving bikes onto the car rack, making the picnic, and carrying it, pitching the tent and so on. Now, I'm game for most things, so I try not to let this put me off, and Alan and I do quite a lot of things together, many of which result in even more work for me! You can't make an omelette without breaking eggs, they say, but I'm way too solid to be breakable.

What do we do? It depends on the weather, of course, and also on the amount of chores I'm sometimes bogged down with, like the housework, shopping, gardening... well, there is only one of me to do all this. Sometimes we go for walks or bike rides. We're lucky enough to have forest quite nearby, with some wonderful trails for walking and cycling and 45 minutes drive away, there is the most enormous reservoir with an eight mile cycle track right the way round it. Whether we walk or bike is determined by how robust I'm feeling and who is most likely to complain. For instance, if we walk, Alan normally starts to complain his legs are aching after about 10 minutes. He will then proceed to complain every step of the way with exactly the same intensity, regardless of how far we walk. If I'm on good form, I can usually withstand this onslaught for a couple of hours. In fact, in the summer we walked right round Holy Island, which is about four miles, with Alan complaining the whole time, but it was a lovely day and I enjoyed myself thoroughly (so did he, really, although he would never admit it!). If we decide to bike, then quite often the proverbial boot is on the other foot. Alan rushes ahead, having the time of his life and has to stop and wait for me, as I puff and blow painfully up every incline. Not that I don't enjoy our bike rides – I do, but I tend to moan rather when the going gets tough and the next day I moan because my bottom/thighs/calves are killing me!

There's nothing I love more than a picnic, which is fortunate really, because we can't afford to eat out very often and, as we're only two, there's never very much picnic to carry. Alan is still fairly neutral about food, unless it contains chocolate or has "sweet" in the name, so picnics are not at the top of his agenda, but he seems to have picked up my love of eating, or not eating in his case, out of doors. Also, we have recently discovered the joys of Enid Blyton's Famous Five, who spend long chunks of each adventure tucking into thick ham and cheese sandwiches and whole fruit cakes as they perch high up on Exmoor, looking for clues and solving mysteries. Alan has begun to appreciate the whole exercise! Sometimes, I think it would be really nice when we go on a country walk, to have a pub lunch on the way, or at the end. But I still don't find it easy to do that sort of thing with just me and Alan, so we reserve it for when we're with friends; the enthusiasm with which I suggest a pint and a ploughman's and proceed to steamroller my friends into the local after a quick trot round the village green has occasionally caused the odd raised eyebrow!

The cinema is a great treat – it's one of the things I love to do and Alan likes it as well, which is lucky. Even more lucky for Alan, but not so much fun for me, is that there are lots of children's films around, particularly during the holidays. However, it is one of the most expensive activities. It costs between £3 and £6 to see a film, but on top of this you have to add the cost of a drink and popcorn; popcorn, which is incredibly cheap to make at home, costs at least £2.50 at the cinema – "small" in this case meaning a bucketful rather than a skip-ful – and a small drink, which must be at least twice the size of Alan's bladder, also costs around £2. So a trip to the pictures, including petrol and parking, comes to around £20 just for the two of us. At least I only have one little mouth to satisfy. I've watched harassed parents with three or four children in tow carefully working out the cost and doling out the popcorn. It's not something we can do every week but occasionally it's worth sacrificing something else for. So we may get to see that latest film, but we probably won't be having pizza that week!

All in all, Alan and I spend quite a lot of time doing things together, just the two of us. Do we get fed up with each other's company? Perhaps, sometimes. One thing I have noticed as Alan gets older is that he is starting to want me to fade into the background, and I've discovered, I'm not very good at it! This year for the first time we went on a package holiday. As usual, I spent far too much time thinking the whole thing through, but eventually I decided we would splash out and go abroad. Alan had never been on an aeroplane before and he'd never been anywhere where he could swim in a swimming pool all day if he liked.

After some searching on the internet, I eventually came across a holiday company which organises packages specifically for one-parent families. I liked the sound of it, because it's hard to interact with other families on a holiday when the adults are all in couples and you're not. It makes you feel like a hanger-on and you inevitably spend huge amounts of time alone. I opted for Majorca, but it was full, so Alan and I ended up in Tunisia in a group of about 15 adults and 25 children. I had had some misgivings – I'm not really a package holiday sort of a person and it was a rather expensive option for us; not that it was a particularly expensive package holiday, as package holidays go, but it cost rather a lot more than our normal camping trips! I was quite pleased with how things turned out.

Alan had lots of other children to play with. He spent practically all day and every day in the swimming pool and had a whale of a time. There was nice company to talk to and I spent hours lying on a sun-bed, chatting, and hearing about other people's lives. At lunchtimes and evenings we all ate together – children at one table, adults at another – and the whole thing was very pleasant; and it was certainly interesting to hear everyone's stories – tales of infidelity and betrayal and a certain amount of bitterness. One woman's husband had recently died suddenly and here she was, bravely starting out again, with two teenagers in tow; one woman was involved in a long-term affair with a married man, who was the father of her child; most had failed marriages: they were more or less the sort of stories one would expect to hear and the everyday details of their lives, for once made me feel how uncomplicated our life is.

What did come as a bit of a shock, though, and probably gave me a foretaste of things to come, was the fact that Alan didn't want to be with me! For the first time I was largely superfluous, except as a provider of coins for the games room and money for drinks. I was very taken aback. In the past, we've always done things together but this, apparently, is something that's not going to last forever! Sooner or later (sooner?), I am not going to be able to rely on my son for company. Already, instead of laughing, Alan has taken to whispering in urgent tones 'Mum – don't do that, it's embarrassing' if I ever sing along to anything or, worse still, if I appear to jig about in any way to the loud ambient music in our local Co-op. I imagine in the future I shall be required to deliver him to activities that I have organised and paid for and, instead of openly watching or even joining in, I shall have to either remain and blend into the background – perhaps some kind of camouflaged clothing will be necessary – or I shall have to leave immediately. And what will I do then? Hang around somewhere waiting for him, or do something else, by myself? Hmm, what would I do?

The holiday in Tunisia gave me the opportunity to consider the differences between my life and the life of a single divorced person. One thing is certain, although I've had to go through a period of very deep self-examination, and although I have to face a lot of difficulties on my own, I'm not operating under the same emotional stress as a parent dealing with rejection and divorce. I haven't had the same sort of emotional shocks. It means that I can focus on Alan, who really needs my emotional support. Most of the children in our group also had another active parent – one they either lived with part time, or one they saw regularly. Many of the divorced parents had whole weekends to themselves – sometimes whole weeks, depending on their arrangements. Most of these adults have had time to think about themselves and build another life outside their family, which is something I have not done, due to a mixture of lack of opportunity and lethargy.

All in all, pleasant and revealing as it was, I won't be able to afford for us to go on such a holiday again for a long time and, even if I could, I don't think I want to spend that much for just one week. Alan is happy to have been on a plane and I'm happy that he's experienced a different culture. We had a great time buying a (very small) carpet, we rode on a camel, we sailed on a ship, we swam in the Mediterranean, Alan got stung by a jelly fish, we visited the local police station to translate for one of the guests who lost a watch (French is one of the languages spoken in Tunisia) and we saw "pirates", one of whom had had both hands chopped off (Alan was very impressed with this!). We "did" Tunisia.

*   *   *

A few weeks after we came back from Tunisia, we drove up to Northumberland, where I did battle with the storm to put up the tent! I can look back on that afternoon and laugh now because, although it was horrible at the time, we went on to have a delightful holiday, the latest in a whole series of lovely times we've had with our tent.

Now, camping as an adult on your own with a child can be a bit complicated. What do you do when you need the loo in the middle of the night, for example? Well, let's just say I'm thankful I remembered to take a bucket with us! It's a versatile piece of equipment, and talking of equipment, you do need a fair amount of stuff to camp in comfort. It does feel like a whole lot of trouble to go to, stuffing all this gear into our tiny car, only to have to take it all out again at the other end, but it's worth being prepared for anything and it isn't very expensive either. After the initial outlay, every year I have "splashed out" on something extra. This year, apart from my new electric pump, I bought a doormat to wipe wet feet on and a plastic box to dump shoes in, so that, for once, the tent wouldn't be full of mud and rainwater. I think I must have been visited by some kind of premonition, because I could never have guessed how much it would rain in Northumberland and my new system of removing shoes was very much put to the test. (It worked, incidentally.) Weather, of course, is an important issue for campers. We've been all over the country – Dorset, Devon, Leicestershire, Suffolk – everywhere we've ever been camping, it has rained. Sometimes I'm tempted to take the tent abroad, but I have a funny feeling that if we crossed the Channel and I managed to cope with the long drive down to the South of France or Spain, that we would still be dogged by rain-clouds. This makes me a rather pessimistic camper, I know, but on the other hand it also makes me a very provident one.

On the campsite in Northumberland, as in Tunisia, Alan was off making friends and playing with them (within sight of the tent) and I was largely left on my own. I tidied up, did bits and pieces, in the evening I poured myself a glass of wine and read the newspaper and my book and I even chatted to some of the other parents on the site – in fact, it wasn't too bad. It was peaceful. Alan was not very far away, so I could keep an eye on him and I had what turned out to be some quality time by myself. It was relaxing not being at home and I was able to switch off. We still did some things together like we always do – rock-pooling, visiting castles, walking – well, me walking, Alan moaning and dragging his poor aching feet! The weather was British and there wasn't a swimming pool. The sea was too cold for anyone under 25. But we both had tremendous fun, we did as we pleased and the whole holiday cost less than a taxi to the airport. So, where are we going next year on our holiday? It's sure to be tent pegs and guy ropes, and me and Alan versus the weather, somewhere in some damp field shrouded with sea mist.

*　*　*

When it rains when we're camping and the weather is generally blustery and cold, we snuggle down on our great airbed, under our warm quilts, we get out puzzle books and reading books and get comfy. The rain thunders on over our heads – I'm confident the tent is waterproof enough to keep us dry – and we feel all the more cosy in our own little home from home. It doesn't feel like a holiday, it feels like an adventure, one that enriches our lives and helps us to appreciate what's valuable in life. I hope that when Alan is older, with a family of his own, he will feel able to take them on the same sort of adventure and carry on the tradition.

I also hope he has to put up the tent in the rain on his own. Then he'll know how I felt!

12

'Are you going to die, Mummy?'

All parents have to face this question sooner or later. As a child starts to wonder about death, it starts to fester in their imaginations until they can't keep it to themselves any longer. When Alan, in the smallest voice, asked me the question at bedtime one evening, I was almost struck dumb, because I wasn't expecting it. I can remember as a child having nightmares about dying and asking my mother the same question. I dare say the answer I gave Alan is the same one my Mum gave me:

> *Alan:*   *Will Millie the cat die one day?*
>
> *Me:*   *One day, yes.*
>
> *Alan:*   *Does everybody die?*
>
> *Me:*   *I'm afraid so, darling.*
>
> *Alan:*   *Are you going to die, Mummy?*
>
> *Me:*   *Yes, one day, but not for a long, long, long time. You don't need to worry about it. I'm not going anywhere yet. You'll be grown up with a family of your own by then.*

*   *   *

Alan announced the other day that he would like a brother or sister. It was just after tea and I was watching "Strictly Come Dancing – it takes two", as usual. I said 'Oh, would you dear?' and left it at that, because there was really no more to be said at the time. I know he said it because he was cross with me. He wanted me to play Monopoly instead of watching the TV. You see, Alan imagines that if he had a brother or sister, they would automatically play with him whenever it suited him. In my experience, both as a sister and as an onlooker, this doesn't necessarily follow and in any case, having another child is something I had already considered and rejected.

Early on, Alan's social worker had asked me if I would consider another child if one became available. I guessed what she was getting at, although she didn't actually say it. What she meant was: 'If Alan's birth mother has another baby which ends up in care, would you consider having it too?' I thought about it. Maybe we would feel more of a family if there were more of us. Perhaps it might be nice to have a little girl as well as a boy – pretty dresses and nice girly games (without mud!) – it was very tempting. Would another child mean that I wouldn't always be the sole focus of Alan's attention? Because, lovely though it is to be the centre of someone's world, just sometimes it would be nice to fade into the background a little!

This last point was borne out just the other day when we had one of Alan's friends round to play. The two boys played brilliantly together all afternoon. I hardly had to intervene at all, and then it was only to offer biscuits and a drink – oh, and once I had to say 'Don't bring my duvet downstairs, please!' 'This is more like it, I thought,' as I managed to get on with tasks that would have been left half done on a normal day, with Alan requiring my attention every five minutes. I shut myself in the kitchen for three solid hours and simply did my own thing at my own pace (ie. slowly), while the boys played with the playstation, built a den and played football outside. It felt wonderful! At five o'clock, though, as interest in football started to dwindle, the boys suddenly began to argue over something small. Quick as a flash, I called out 'Boys, it's time for James to go home – come in and get cleaned up.' So just as things looked as if they might turn nasty, Alan's friend James was whisked away home with promises of coming to play another day and everything ended well. If James were a sibling, we'd have been stuck with him!

Annie has two boys, so shortly after Alan arrived on the scene when his social worker brought up the issue of another child, I asked Annie what she thought:

> Me: *Is it easier with two children?*
>
> Annie: *I think it's probably easier with two sometimes. They do occupy each other and play football together and so on.*
>
> Me: *Do they argue?*
>
> Annie: *Well, yes they do and sometimes it's constant bickering, which is awful. It can ruin your day!*
>
> Me: *Do you think I should consider having another child?*
>
> Annie: *No, I don't. I don't think Alan would cope with sharing you at all!*

*   *   *

On balance I agreed and five years down the line, I still agree. Since Alan said he wanted a brother or sister, though, I felt I should at least give it some further thought. I came up with these points: first, I'm pushing fifty – have I got the energy for another child? probably not; second, I'm broke nearly all the time as it is – could I afford another mouth to feed (shoes, camping equipment for one more, clothes and Christmas presents)? definitely not; third, is Alan secure enough and confident enough to share me with another child, even after all this time? I don't think so, and right now, I'm not prepared to risk it.

This chapter is not going to be all doom and gloom, despite the chapter heading, but it's about the future of my family – that's Alan and me – and the future necessarily contains bits we would rather avoid. I don't normally think about it very much, although I probably should. I'm often so caught up with what's going on in our everyday lives that my plan for the day tends to be: wake up, do your best, head for the end of the day, go to bed (normally in that order, but not always). I suppose I usually manage to plan a week ahead. Sometimes I plan a month ahead. I think about where we might go on holiday, although that probably qualifies more as escapism than actual planning. I save for Christmas (well, I attempt to) and I organise birthdays in advance. But I don't sit and consider "the future" much.

So, what shape will our family be in the future? Well, having more or less ruled out another child, the other possibility is that I might meet someone and want to marry him. To be honest, this feels like such a remote possibility that I can hardly be bothered to address it. However, I suppose I can't totally rule it out, even though I don't have enough energy to make conversation some days, let alone dazzle anyone with my sparkling repartee. Alan, we know, would love to have a daddy in theory, so I shall try to keep an open mind.

Will we manage to avoid financial ruin in the future? I hope so. As Alan grows older and is out at school longer, I shall be able to work more and earn more money. I'm expecting him to be more expensive as he grows up, and I definitely intend to be more expensive as I grow old. We will be comfortable, rather than rich – unless I either win the lottery or manage to dazzle that millionaire. I imagine in ten years' time we shall still be living in the same house and, who knows, I may have managed to weed the garden by then! Alan will need me less and less and hopefully I shall have started to expand my own life again to fill the

119

inevitable gaps he will leave.

One of the worst-case scenarios, of course, is if something should happen to me. It's not an easy subject to broach light-heartedly, but death is inevitable and known for causing the maximum of inconvenience by happening without warning at just the wrong time, so it's something to be carefully considered. While you are waiting to adopt, you are required to say who will have your child if you die; and for a single parent, it's a pressing issue, because there isn't a second parent to simply step into the breach. Obviously it's an issue you discuss with your social worker, but it's hard to approach potential surrogate parents when you're talking purely hypothetically about a hypothetical child. Can you seriously expect friends or family to agree to take on a child they don't know? Early on I discussed it with Annie :

> Me: *I've been asked to think about who would have my child if anything happened to me. It's not been very easy.*
>
> Annie: *No, it isn't easy. We had the same problem, but have a reciprocal agreement with my sister. She'd have the boys if anything happened to us and we'd have her boys if anything happened to her.*
>
> Me: *How would you feel if I asked you and Matt if you'd be prepared to take my child on?*
>
> Annie: *It's a different situation. We're not family, for one thing, so I don't think we'd be allowed to have him or her. Also, I think having a small child would be very difficult, depending on the child. I don't think it would be fair on our boys.*
>
> Me: *No, I can see that. It's tricky isn't it? But I think it's better to be honest about it.*

I quite understood.

* * *

So what would happen if the worst happened? Well, financially, there wouldn't be any problems because, like many people, ultimately I'm worth more dead than alive – at least in monetary terms, which is a sobering thought!

I considered asking my parents, but they were already in their seventies and, whilst I know I could rely on them to do the best they could, it didn't seem fair to lumber them with a small child at their age. Which brings me to the nub of the problem for many single adopters and that is, we just don't have enough family; only one set of siblings and one set of grandparents. I asked my single adopter friend Carol how she'd coped with it:

> Me: *What provisions have you made for your son if anything should happen to you?*
>
> Carol: *Well, fortunately, my sister has children of her own of about the same age. She was always very supportive of the idea of me adopting, so she was happy to agree to have him, even before she'd met him or knew anything about him.*
>
> Me: *That's incredibly good of her. You're lucky to have her on your side. What would you have done if she hadn't agreed?*
>
> Carol: *I'm not sure. I don't really know…*

* * *

I didn't really know, either, but I think one thing is clear, if you're planning to be a single adopter, you need to try and think the matter through, unpleasant though it is to dwell on your own death, and remote as it may seem.

Finally, I approached my brother. He is divorced, with no children and has a busy life – he has two jobs, writes music and studies – he's an all-round good bloke, and he agreed that he would be responsible for Alan. At this point, he's probably thinking 'I don't remember agreeing to that!' but he did, and I'm happy that he did, because he's a very sensible, caring individual (flattery, you see!) and I know I can trust him to make the right decisions and to make sure Alan has all he needs. Without his agreement, though I am fit and well, I don't think I would have felt as easy going ahead with the adoption.

I realise I may not be typical of all individuals considering single adoption. I recognise that I have had some advantages: I had a very well paid job before I started out and I owned my home. I had a decent employer with generous adoption leave and redundancy policies. These things helped. But if you don't have these advantages it doesn't mean you're not suitable to adopt. The adoption services aren't looking for perfect situations. They're looking for ordinary people who can offer a stable loving home to a child who needs a family. Parenthood is a great leveller; we all get tired, we all worry about our children and we all have to face the fact that we may not be around forever.

*   *   *

Now, Alan knows a bit about death and dying. Last year at Easter, the vicar visited his school and described in what some might call excessively graphic detail about how Jesus was nailed to the cross and had a sword poked in his side. I believe there was a discussion about blood, divine and otherwise, and some parents were quite upset when their horrified progeny returned home with tales of death and destruction reminiscent of a video nasty. Alan was able to act it out quite impressively. I don't think he was unduly upset by it, for he has been wielding a sword ever since he was old enough to pick up a stick and wave it. I don't think I can be held responsible for his preoccupation with violence, as I don't allow him to watch violent films and I actively discourage fighting. I guess some of it has been picked up from Harry Potter and Robin Hood on TV and some has been learned in the playground.

Suffice it to say, Alan is now aware that people die,

although he hasn't quite got to grips with the finality of death yet, and the Easter story certainly didn't help him with that! In any case, Alan seems to rather like pretending he's been shot or stabbed and loves to sway and crash to his knees, squirming and groaning, hands clutched to his stomach (I remember my brother doing the same when we were little), only to jump up and start fighting all over again. Boys will be boys, I guess! And he has very definite views about what he wants for the future:

> Me: *What do you want to do when you grow up, Alan?*
>
> Alan: *I want to be a fish seller.*
>
> Me: *What, in a fish and chip shop?*
>
> Alan: *Nooooo, silly! I mean a man who sells pet fish.*
>
> Me: *Where will you get the fish from?*
>
> Alan: *I'll go diving in the sea and scoop them all up in a big net.*
>
> Me: *What about rugby?*
>
> Alan: *Well, I want to be a famous rugby player.*
>
> Me: *That would be nice. You could be on "Strictly Come Dancing" then, like Matt Dawson.*
>
> Alan: *Yeah!*

* * *

Normally, Alan is quite gung ho, so I can only imagine how he must have been feeling when he barely whispered the question about Mummy dying that evening, and seeing how frightened he was, what could I say? His sense of security is so fragile and his need for the truth is so great. In retrospect, I should have said that he had a shining future ahead of him, that he was so loved he would always be OK, that Mummy would always be with him, one way or another. Instead, I stroked his hair and I crossed my fingers and hoped, for both our sakes, that what I had said would turn out to be true.

EPILOGUE
What's it really like?

I've now been a single parent for quite some time and, as an "old" hand (not so much of the "old", thank you!), I've been asked to talk to other women – and men – who are thinking about adoption and want to know what it's "really like" to adopt without a partner. It's a difficult question to answer because, as I know from my own experience, it's hard to hear and understand what life will be like as a single parent of an adopted child until you're there. Besides, you don't want to put people off by being too brutally frank; and all children are different, as are all parents. But just in case it's helpful and hoping I won't frighten anyone away, here are my top tips:

Think carefully about why you want to become a parent; adoption is about what's best for the child, not what's convenient for you. Children who have to be separated from their birth families are not meant to fill a gap in our lives.

Never apologise for being a single parent. Look for an agency that welcomes single people and has experience of placing children in one-parent families. You should never feel that they would have preferred you to be one of a couple. Don't be afraid to ask them to put you in touch with other single adopters, for example. If you're comfortable with being single, then your child will be comfortable with it too.

Be prepared for your life to change radically. Don't think you'll be able to simply slip an adopted child into your life and carry on as normal. Talk to as many single adopters as you can, but also to one-parent birth families. There may be differences in your family circumstances, but they will understand many of the challenges that you will face and where to go to get help.

Sort out your financial situation before you commit yourself. Nothing is cheaper for two than for one, especially if one of you breaks and loses things, tears clothes and grows larger at an alarming rate! You don't need to be rich to be a single parent, but you do need to be able to maintain a comfortable lifestyle. Think hard about whether or not you'll be able to carry on working and, if you can't carry on with your job, carefully think through how you're going to earn money to support your new family. There is a single parent adviser at my local Job Centre. Check out yours!

Build up a network of support among friends, relations and neighbours. Keep them interested and involved. I can't tell you how important this is. Sometimes it's hard to ask for help, even from those closest to you, so make sure the people you rely on are ready to support you in a crisis. You don't have anything to prove, so don't be afraid to admit you need help. We all do – well, I do, that's for sure! For your own peace of mind, agree with your relatives who will look after your adopted child if the worst should happen to you – it's tricky, but essential, and it will make you feel better.

Grow a thicker skin and develop your laughter muscles! The best way to deal with other people's lack of tact and understanding is to have a good laugh about it. It's hard to be held responsible for your child's misdemeanours, harder still if you can't go home and let off steam to a partner, so phone a friend with a good sense of humour and poke fun at the situation. It'll help you put it all into perspective. The odd glass of wine helps, too!

Buy a good aluminium stepladder and a wheelbarrow! You will be surprised at how much more fixing, mending, decorating and lifting of heavy things has to be done once you're a family unit. And while you are at it, develop a special skill like putting up a large tent on your own or changing a wheel at the roadside – your child may even help, and onlookers will be full of admiration (or you could do what I did and use your Tesco Clubcard vouchers to join the RAC. I think that was extremely resourceful of me!).

Keep a life of your own. This is easier said than done and requires a lot of effort at times when you'd just like to collapse in a heap in front of the telly. But it's worth it, because children don't stay in the nest forever, and you will have a lot of living to do after they leave home. Don't be afraid of giving your wholehearted attention to a child who needs the security and stability of a loving family, but remember that you won't be able to be a good parent, with a proper sense of perspective, if your whole life revolves around your child. You'll also be very boring and won't be invited to parties!

Don't rush into anything. Always have a plan, and

always have a plan B. So, whether you're going shopping, drawing money out of the bank, planning a trip, or a day out, or simply spending the day at home with your child, be proactive. In my experience, every time I just "let things happen" things seem to go wrong. So, even though it's a drag at times, think ahead about what you're doing. It'll help you relax and enjoy life, honest!

No one is going to tell you that adopting on your own is easy – because it isn't. Is it worth it, though? Yes, most definitely. I have a happy and loving little boy to share my life with. It's like having sunshine every day! So if you're considering adopting on your own and, after reading all this you still feel you can do it, my advice is 'Go for it'. You won't regret it.

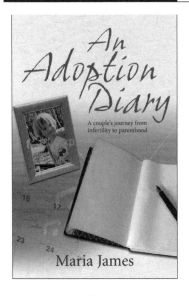
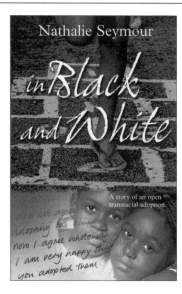